You can return this item to any library but please
note that not all libraries are open every day.
Items must be returned on or before the due date.
Failure to do so will result in overdue charges.
Items may be renewed unless requested by
another customer, in person or by telephone, on
two occasions only. Your membership card
number will be required.
Please look after this item – you may be charged
for any damage.

BOURNEMOUTH LIBRARIES
Headquarters: Leisure & Tourism Directorate
Town Hall, Bournemouth, BH2 6DY

D0540695

ROMANTIC CROCHET

30 Beautiful Projects for your Home

RHODA ROBERTSON

CAXTON EDITIONS

ACKNOWLEDGEMENTS

For me, this book on crochet lace is a dream come true, a chance to pass on my ideas to like-minded people. My most grateful thanks to Ena McKeeman for checking all my patterns and diagrams so thoroughly and with such accuracy, to Vivien Oliver, my sister, whose nimble fingers hammered endlessly at the computer, converting my notes into legible text, to Julie Matthews for her constructive ideas and clever ways with words and to all the other ladies who gave their time and help so generously. I am much indebted to my crochet students for testing the patterns and producing some of the crochet items included in this book, especially Moira Dow, Daphne Fretwell, Catherine Aitken, Jan Heriot and Jennifer Thomson. A special thanks to my friends Sylvia Cosh and James Walters for their help and guidance, to Munni Srivastava of Savitri Books, the sole orchestrator of this book, whose good planning at every stage made it all possible. Cheerful Odile Noël, 'translator extraordinaire', I thank you too. My gratitude also to my family and friends for their encouragement and good humour over the many months of hard work. Finally, a huge thank you to my husband Stuart for his patience, understanding and support during my time-out from other 'pleasures' (such as housework) and for giving me confidence throughout.

Rhoda Robertson

Savitri Books extend their cordial thanks to Anne and Roddy Dewe for allowing their lovely house to be a 'location'.

A Savitri Books Publication

First published in Great Britain in 1998
by Savitri Books Ltd
115J Cleveland Street
London W1P 5PN

This edition published 2002 by Caxton Editions
an imprint of The Caxton Publishing Group

© 1998, Savitri Books (this edition and all photographs)
© 1998, Rhoda Robertson (text, diagrams and projects)

ISBN 1 8406742 0 2

Art direction and design by Mrinalini Srivastava
Photography by Sarah Dewe

Typeset in 11/14 Sabon
Reproduced by Regent Publishing Services, Hong Kong
Printed and bound by **Star Standard Industries Pte Ltd**

IMPORTANT NOTICES

The author and publishers advise the readers of this book to photocopy the diagrams which accompany each project. These can be enlarged to facilitate the reading of the symbols and each row coloured as the work proceeds. However, the author and publishers advise readers to take careful note of the photocopying and copyright reproduction laws that apply to other sources of designs. The projects contained in this book are all original designs and are the property of the author. Anyone wanting to use these designs, wholly or partly, for commercial purposes, should seek permission from the copyright owners.

The author and publishers of this book have made every effort to ensure that the instructions contained in the book are accurate and complete. They cannot, however, be responsible for human error, typographical mistakes or variations in individual work.

CONTENTS

INTRODUCTION

Ever since I was around fifteen years old and sat spellbound as my aunt was teaching me how to crochet, I have been fascinated by the diversity of patterns and textures which can be created with a few simple stitches. Since then, I am seldom without my hooks and yarns and I find it difficult to resist the temptation to pick up my hook and work just another few rows...

Over the years I have experimented with texture, colour and pattern and much of my work has been exhibited. I have always had a strong commitment to promote textile crafts and I was fortunate to have the opportunity to do so through craft guilds, exhibitions, displays and workshops across my native Scotland. One of my greatest joys is to pass on my knowledge and experience to others in the workshops and courses I teach. It is always exciting to meet other enthusiasts who share my passion for crochet. Their eagerness to learn has been an encouragement and an inspiration. For several years, I have had the privilege of judging for the Handcraft Section of the Royal Highland Show in Edinburgh, a prestigious open competition which attracts entries of a very high standard, world-wide.

The collection of lace crochet projects contained in this book represents some of my recent work, but also includes some of my students' favourites. There is, I hope, something to please everyone, with projects ranging in size and complexity and using a variety of lace techniques. The romantic charm of this fascinating craft has been adapted to suit contemporary taste and you will experience the thrill of creating small personal treasures, attractive gifts for someone special or items for your own home – tomorrow's family heirlooms.

A BRIEF HISTORY OF CROCHET

Very little is known of the origins of crochet; some say it originated in Biblical times, maybe as long ago as 950 BC, during the days of Solomon. Fragments of crochet work have been found in Egypt and in ancient Babylon which was a wool trade centre. The Babylonians were fond of elaborate woollen clothes and it is more than likely that these were knitted or crocheted. Ancient crochet patterns found in the Middle East and North Africa suggest that crochet has been around for thousands of years.

'Shepherd's knitting' is a delightful term which was used long ago in Scotland. Sheep's wool caught on fencing and bushes was gathered by the shepherds and, after spinning into a rough wool, it would be made into simple garments, using a stick with a crude hook carved at one end. Crochet has come a long way since then!

The rapid mechanisation of the weaving process affected some of the traditional methods of producing fabrics such as crochet and knitting, which suffered badly and almost died out. For a long time crochet was made by nuns and was confined behind the walls of convents. In early 19th-century Britain, however, lace trimmings were becoming fashionable and crochet was revived as a suitable accomplishment for well-to-do young ladies. The new mills now spun fine cotton yarn which offered new possibilities for the exponents of the craft. Around the same time, crochet in Ireland became an important cottage industry and ever since, Irish crochet has really been a craft in its own right.

The Victorian period witnessed the ever-growing popularity of crochet. Contemporary paintings and photographs of Victorian interiors show how every available surface – furniture, shelves, the piano even – was covered with doilies, antimacassars and flounces made of crochet lace. The enthusiasm for the craft generated an enormous wealth of designs and intricate patterns. If you have a textile museum near you, it is well worth a visit, as the wonderful work of days-gone-by can be a great source of inspiration to the modern maker. The tablecloth on the frontispiece of this book was made at the turn of the century and inspired the pattern of the one shown on page 95.

BEFORE YOU START

At the beginning of each project you will find one of the following symbols:

They indicate the degree of complexity of the particular project. One crochet hook indicates a good starting project, two hooks are for the fairly experienced worker and three accompany projects which represent more of a challenge. Although this book is not primarily designed for the complete newcomer to the craft, all the projects are fully explained and are sufficiently varied to appeal to a wide range of ability. Choose your first project carefully and you will soon gain the experience and the confidence required to tackle the more complex designs.

WORKING NOTES

◆ Tension / Gauge

It is important to make a sample before you embark on your chosen project, as it is the only way to check whether the tension / gauge (the number of stitches and/or spaces over a given measurement) is correct. An incorrect or uneven tension means that the finished piece of work will be smaller or larger than the desired size or that the work will not lie flat. If the sample is smaller and tighter than it should be, try using a larger hook; if it is bigger or looser, use a smaller hook. When a pattern does not specify a tension check, refer to the finished size of the object to guide

you. Beginners often have problems with uneven tension. This will be corrected by practice.

◆ Quantities of crochet thread

Most of the projects in this book were worked using DMC Cébélia crochet cotton No 10 thickness and a 1.50 mm crochet hook. Some can also be made using a No 20 cotton thread with a 1.25 mm crochet hook, which produce a smaller version of the project. The amounts given are sufficient to allow for slight differences in tension or size of hook which may influence the quantity of thread required. Some of the smaller items use such a small amount of thread that it is difficult to specify accurately. You may be able to make several items from one small ball. If you substitute a different brand of cotton, you should note that a No 10 can vary in weight and texture from one manufacturer to another. Check your tension carefully and make sure you have sufficient yarn to complete the pattern, as two batches of cotton may vary considerably in colour.

◆ DIAGRAMS

All the projects in this book are accompanied by one or several diagrams. These are based on symbols which represent the various stitches (see the list of abbvreviations and symbols and crochet terms on page 10). Familiarise yourself with them if you are a beginner. They provide a visual way of checking the number of stitches at a glance. Even if you are not used to working from diagrams, do give them a try as they are an invaluable aid to checking the accuracy of your work. It is important to read through to the end of the pattern before you begin and to refer to the diagram as you work. As you tackle each row or round, always read to the end of the instruction before you start, as the beginning and the finish are usually different from the middle section. Make a photocopy of the diagrams, enlarging them if necessary, as it has not always been possible to fit all the written instructions next to the relevant diagram. Colour each row or round as you work to keep track of where you are.

ABBREVIATIONS & SYMBOLS

This is a list of abbreviated crochet terms as used in the written instructions for the projects included in this book. The symbols identify the various stitches used within the diagrams. **This glossary is not exhaustive but includes solely the stitches actually used in this book.**

chain = ch

chains = chs

slip stitch = sl st

double crochet = dc

half treble = htr

treble = tr

double treble = dtr

stitch or stitches = st or sts

spaces or spaces = sp or sps

block or blocks = blk or blks

turning chain = tch

yarn over hook = yoh

fasten off

rejoin or start

row or round direction

linking points

POINTS TO REMEMBER

- Asterisks * in a series of instructions denote a part of the pattern to be repeated.

- Brackets ( ) represent a series of stitches to be worked into a stitch, space or loop, a specified number of times.

- The diagrams in this book always show the right side of the work.

- The numbers written in **bold** characters at the centre of the circular diagrams denote the number of starting chains. The other figures denote the **row** or **round** number, or the number of ch stitches whithin a pattern, e.g. loops or spaces.

- The loop on the hook is referred to as the **working loop** and is never counted as a chain stitch. After completing a stitch or group of stitches, there should be only one loop on the hook – **the working loop.**

- Always insert the hook under the top two threads of the stitch, unless otherwise stated.

- **Right side – wrong side.** Due to the way in which the thread is twisted during the work, slight differences appear in the upper and the underside of the piece. When several pieces of work must be joined, great care must be taken not to confuse the two sides. Marking the wrong side with a contrasting thread is good practice.

- Both Imperial and metric measurements are given in this book. Work to one or the other.

EQUIVALENT ENGLISH AND AMERICAN TERMS

There are differences between English and American crochet terms. To avoid confusion, refer to the conversion chart on page 109.

CROCHET STITCHES USED IN THIS BOOK

All crochet begins with a slip loop or a knot, followed by the required number of chain stitches. To make a slip loop, fold a short length of yarn to make a loop, insert hook into this loop and catch the long end of the thread, draw through (diagram 1) and tighten, till the loop slides easily along the hook (diagram 2). The slip loop is not a stitch but is referred to as the working loop.

DIAGRAM 1   DIAGRAM 2

Chain stitch (ch st). Yarn over hook (yoh) and draw it through the loop on the hook – one ch st is made (diagram 1). Continue till required number of ch sts are made (diagram 2). This is called the starting or foundation chain.

DIAGRAM 1   DIAGRAM 2

Slip stitch (sl st). Work a short chain. Insert hook in the second ch from the hook under the top two threads of ch st (diagram 1), yoh and draw yarn through ch st and the remaining loop on the hook (diagram 2). One sl st is made.

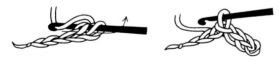

DIAGRAM 1   DIAGRAM 2

Double crochet (dc). Work a short ch. Always make sure you are working into the front / right side of the ch. Insert hook in second ch from hook, under the top two threads of ch st, leaving a single thread underneath the hook (diagram 1).

DIAGRAM 1

Yoh and draw yarn back through ch st, 2 loops on the hook. Yoh and draw through the remaining 2 loops on hook (diagram 2). One dc is made (diagram 3).

DIAGRAM 2   DIAGRAM 3

Half treble (htr). Yoh, insert hook in third ch from hook (diagram 1), yoh and draw yarn back through ch st, pulling yarn up slightly, 3 loops on hook. Yoh and draw through all 3 loops on hook (diagram 2). One htr is made (diagram 3).

DIAGRAM 1   DIAGRAM 2

DIAGRAM 3

TREBLE (tr)

Yoh, insert hook in fourth ch from hook (diagram 1), yoh and draw yarn back through ch st, pulling yarn up slightly, 3 loops on hook (diagram 2). Yoh and draw through two loops only, yoh again and draw through remaining two loops (diagram 3). One tr is made (diagram 4).

DIAGRAM 1   DIAGRAM 2

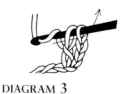 

DIAGRAM 3   DIAGRAM 4

Double treble (dtr). Yoh twice, insert hook in 5th chain from hook (diagram 1), yoh and draw back through ch st, pulling yarn up slightly, 4 loops on hook. *yoh and draw through 2 loops only (diagram 2). Repeat from* 2 more times (diagram 3 and 4), till one loop remains. One dtr is made (diagram 5).

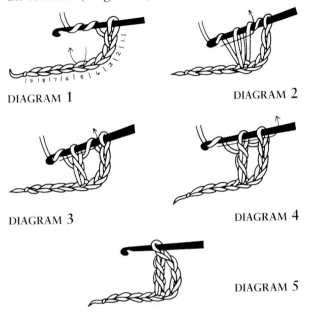

DIAGRAM **1**   DIAGRAM **2**

DIAGRAM **3**   DIAGRAM **4**

DIAGRAM **5**

FILET CROCHET

Filet crochet is the name given to regular open network (or mesh) worked in fine cotton – (usually in one colour) – using trs and chs. The designs are produced by 'filling in' some of the spaces with trebles, called blocks (blks) and leaving other spaces open to create the pattern. Maintaining a firm and even tension throughout is very important. The blocks should be fairly solid to show the design to the best effect. Change hook size till you get the correct tension. In the patterns which accompany the projects in this book, the blks are represented by the symbol X , the spaces are left blank.

There are two ways of producing the mesh, each creating a slightly different effect. These differ in the number of chs used to produce the mesh or open sps and the number of tr used to form the blks. The particular method used is specified with each pattern. Make sure you use the correct one.

Method 1 (probably the most commonly used) consists of 2ch sps between 4tr blks. The finished work will be square with a fairly open texture.

Method 2 consists of 1ch sp between 3tr blks. The spaces in the mesh are rectangular and the finished work has a closer texture (diagram 2).

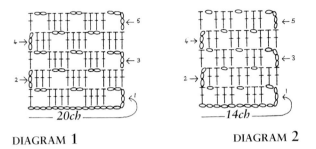

DIAGRAM **1**   DIAGRAM **2**

WORKING IN THE ROUND (using the sl st)

The same basic stitches are used when working in a circle, but the starting ch is joined by a slip stitch (sl st) to form a ring. Once the ring is formed, the motif or circular pattern is worked from the centre outward, increasing the number of stitches on each round to keep the work flat. At the start of each new round ch sts are worked to equal the height of the stitches being used on the next round. These are the equivalent of 'turning chains' and may be counted as a stitch.

To form a ring, work the required number of ch sts, insert hook in the first ch st made, yoh and draw through ch st **and** the remaining loop on the hook (diagram 1). One sl st is made and the starting ring is formed (diagram 2). At the start of the first round, work the required number of ch sts to equal the height of sts on the first round. Work the stitches into the ring, **not** into the ch sts (diagram 3). To complete the first round, work a sl st into the top of the turning chain at the beginning of the round (diagram 4).

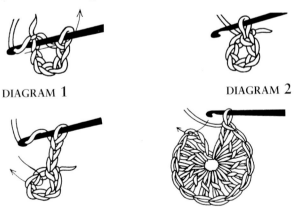

DIAGRAM **1**   DIAGRAM **2**

DIAGRAM **3**   DIAGRAM **4**

STITCHES FOR SPECIAL EFFECTS

3ch picot
Work 3ch, sl st into the 3rd ch from hook, pull tight.

4ch picot
Work 4ch, sl st into 4th ch from hook, pull tight.

5ch picot
Work 5ch, sl st into 5th ch from hook, pull tight.

5 loop puff st
It is worked using extended htrs as follows: *yoh, insert hook into st, catch thread, draw through a long loop, up to ¼ in / 6 mm, 3 loops on hook, Repeat from* 4 more times in the same stitch. Finally, catch the thread and draw firmly through all 11 loops. A tight ch st may be added after the puff st to secure.

Double crochet (dc) variation
Work as a basic dc, but insert the hook in the back single thread only to create a ridged effect.

Treble (tr) variation
Work as a basic tr, but insert the hook in the back single thread only to create a ridged effect. This technique can also be used with htrs and dtrs. The ridges will appear on the right side of the work.

TO INCREASE

Increase 2dc
2 complete dc together in 1 stitch.

Increase 3dc
3 complete dc together in 1 stitch.

Increase 2htr
2 complete htr together in 1 stitch.

Increase 3htr
3 complete htr together in 1 stitch.

Increase 2tr
2 complete tr together in 1 stitch.

Increase 3tr
3 complete tr together in 1 stitch.

Increase 2dtr
2 complete dtr together in 1 stitch.

Increase 3dtr
3 complete dtr together in 1 stitch.

TO DECREASE

Decrease 2dc
hook in the first st, catch thread, draw loop through, hook in next st, catch thread, draw loop through, catch thread again and draw through all 3 loops on hook.

Decrease 3dc
as above, but work over 3 separate sts, finally taking the thread through all 4 loops on the hook.

Decrease 2htr

1htr worked to first stage (3 loops on hook), 1htr in next st to first stage (5 loops on hook), catch thread, draw through all 5 loops on hook.

Decrease 3htr

as above, but work over 3 separate sts, taking thread through all 7 loops on hook.

Decrease 2tr

1tr worked to last stage but one (2 loops on hook), 1tr in next to last stage but one (3 loops on hook), catch thread and draw through all 3 loops on hook.

Decrease 3tr

as above, but work over 3 separate sts, taking thread through all 4 loops on hook.

Decrease 2dtr

1dtr worked to last stage but one (2 loops on hook) 1dtr in next st to last stage but one (3 loops on hook), catch thread and draw through all 3 loops on hook.

Decrease 3dtr

as above, but work over 3 separate sts, finally taking thread through all 4 loops on hook.

WORKING NOTES

◆ To **fasten off** and secure the last stitch, cut the thread at approximately 6 in / 15 cm from the **working loop,** draw tail end back through loop and pull gently till tight.

◆ Always leave a good length of thread when you make the slip loop at the start of the foundation chain. If you reach the end of the first row to discover that you are short of chain stitches, simply remove the hook from the loop and insert it into the first ch, pull the thread through and add the required number of chs, plus one extra. Pull the tail end through the last ch loop to fasten off. Now continue the pattern.

◆ **Turning chains** are used to move on to the next row or round. The number of turning chains used is usually equivalent to the height of the first stitch at the start of the next row or round, 1 or 2ch for a double crochet; 2ch for a half treble; 3ch for a treble. In some cases, especially with longer stitches, the turning chain is counted as a stitch. This is specified in the instructions for each project.

◆ **Problems with the starting chain.** If you have too many chs at the end of the first row, disregard them and carefully unpick them when the project is complete or oversew them into the back of the work. If the starting chain always turns out to be too tight and difficult to work into, try using a larger hook to make the starting chain, returning to the original hook size for the remainder of the pattern. Similarly, work the starting chain with a smaller hook, if it tends to be loose

◆ **Joining yarns.** A join should be almost invisible and not create an unsightly lump in the work. This is even more important with crochet lace. If possible, make the join close to a solid part of the design or near the edge, rather than in the middle of an open mesh section.

There are two ways of joining thread of the same colour:

1. Before finishing the ball of cotton, while there are still some 6 in / 15 cm left, take the beginning of the new ball, tie the two tail ends together and tighten the knot. Pull the tails through to the wrong side of the work and carefully sew in both ends separately.

2. Insert the hook into the next stitch, pull the loop through from the old ball and finish the stitch by dropping the thread from the old ball. Catch the tail end from the new ball to complete the stitch, pull both tails firmly to the wrong side of the work and darn each thread separately, in different directions.

ADVICE TO LEFT-HANDERS

As most crocheters are right-handed, the diagrams have been drawn to suit them. If you are left-handed, there are ways of transferring the diagrams. The traditional method is to stand the book up and hold a square mirror at right angles to the page. This is a little awkward, but it will give you a reversed image to work from. A far better solution is to use a photocopier to print the design on tracing paper. Turn the paper over to follow the reversed working diagram, any figures appearing on the diagram can then be viewed from the right side of the copy. The written instructions remain the same.

AFTERCARE OF CROCHET LACE

All the projects in this book are made in pure cotton thread which is a very resistant material. A gentle hand wash is recommended, using pure soap flakes or a mild liquid detergent. Rinse well. Do not wring. Absorb the excess water by spreading the item over a large towel, roll up carefully and press gently down with your hands. A slight shrinkage may occur but, while the lace is still damp, it is possible to ease the work back to its original size by pulling it gently and evenly by hand or by pinning it out and allowing it to dry in position. This process is known as blocking.

Stubborn stains on white cotton items, can usually be removed by steeping the piece for twenty minutes in a bleach solution (use 1 tablespoonful of bleach to 2 pints / 1 litre of tepid water).

BLOCKING & IRONING

If the work does not require washing, it should be steam-pressed lightly on the wrong side, using a damp cloth. Washed pieces should be left on a thick towel, till almost dry. Cover a large piece of cardboard with cling film. Draw a template of the outer shape of the article on a piece of plain paper (tinted paper is even better under a piece made of white cotton thread). Use a compass for circular pieces. Graph paper is ideal for square or oblong designs. Slip this template under the cling film and pin in place at the corners. Right side facing, ease the work till it fits the drawn shape, then pin out using stainless steel pins. Do not overstretch the work. Once the main shape is set in place, open out the picots, pull out all points gently, ease the loops and curves making sure they match all round. Use as many pins as necessary. If the work begins to dry out before the pinning is finished, dampen it lightly using a water spray. Leave to dry completely before removing the pins. With filet crochet, make sure that all the blocks and spaces are square and well aligned, and that all edges are straight. The blocking process should be repeated each time the article is washed.

Crochet work can benefit from a light starching. Spray starch available in cans gives very good results and is easier to use than conventional starch.

SEWING INSTRUCTIONS FOR THE TISSUE BOX LINING & FOR THE POCHETTE
(See pages 85 and 58, respectively.)

B

B

A

A

sewing line

9¼ in /
25 cm

*Opening at the top of the box.
Trace with a fabric pencil and
cut <u>after</u> completing the
assembly of the lining. Finish
off with toning bias binding.*

14½ in /
37 cm

– 5 in / 13 cm –

5/8 in
15 mm

A

A

*When the lining is
finished, attach point
A to point B with a
few slip stitches.*

B

B

OPPOSITE: PATTERN FOR THE TISSUE BOX LINING (see page 85)
Enlarge this pattern by 200%. Cut twice. Right sides together, pin the two layers together. Machine-stitch, leaving a 2 in / 4 cm gap for turning the work. Trim off excess cloth. Clip the seam in the angles down to the sewing line. Press. Slip stitch the gap. Cut out the top opening and neaten the edges with bias binding.

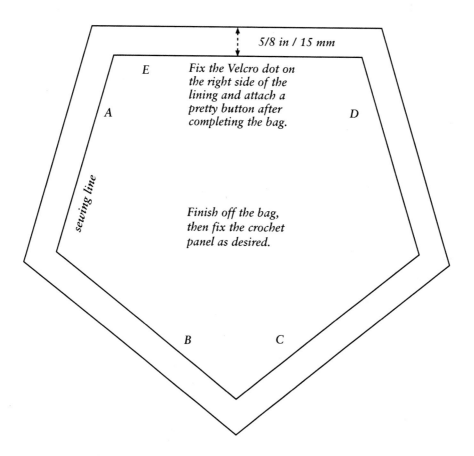

ABOVE: PATTERN FOR THE POCHETTE (see page 58)
Enlarge this pattern by 200%. Cut twice out of the top fabric and twice out of the lining material. Right sides together, pin the two sides of the pochette. Machine-stitch along the sewing lines from A to D. Repeat for the lining. Cut off the excess fabric. Clip the angles down to the sewing line. Turn out the bag and its lining. Press. Fold the top of the pochette along the sewing line. Repeat for the lining. Press. Insert the lining inside the bag. Pin and slip-stich the lining to the top of the bag. Press. Fix the Velcro dot to the lining. Attach the lace panel to the front of the bag and add a pretty button.

Overleaf. The red cushion is produced by using nine of the motifs which are used to form the table mat, see page 21.

TABLE MATS & MATCHING COASTERS

Each table mat is made up of six identical motifs, joined together and framed by a large border. The coaster consists of a single motif, with a narrow edge. One such motif could also be appliqued in the corner of a napkin. Nine of these squares were worked in bright red cotton and were used to form the top of the handsome cushion, shown opposite. This panel was appliqued over a cover made of bright red toning silk and finished off with small tassels. Make up your own cushion or applique the panel over a toning or contrasting ready-made cover.

Approximate sizes: Coaster – 1 motif, including edging: 5 in / 13 cm square. Table mat – 6 motifs, including edging: 16½ x 12½ in / 42 x 32 cm. Cushion – 9 motifs: 15 x 15 in / 38 x 38 cm

MATERIALS. Table mat and coaster: 75 g DMC Cébélia crochet cotton No 10 – white 5200. Cushion: 100 g DMC Cébélia crochet cotton No 10 – red 816, a 1.50 mm crochet hook, an 18 in / 46 cm cushion pad

WORKING NOTES

◆ Always check number of ch sts on every round, especially from round 7 (see diagram 1, page 20).
◆ Rounds 7, 8, 9 and 10. Please note the second sl st at the ends of these rounds, before the start of the next round.
◆ On round 9, the dc is worked over and around, incorporating the ch sts from the previous two rounds.
◆ Refer to the stitch diagram as you work, making a photocopy is helpful.

TO MAKE ONE MOTIF

(excluding edge): 6ch, sl st to form a ring (see diagram 1, **first motif**).

Round 1   2ch (to count as 1dc), 7dc in ring (8dc altogether), sl st to 2ch to complete round.

Round 2   7ch, 1tr in next dc, *4ch, 1tr in next dc, repeat from* 5 more times. End with 4ch, sl st to 3rd of 7ch at the beginning of the round (8sps).

Round 3   3ch (to count as 1tr), 2tr at the base of 3ch, *4ch, miss 4ch, 3tr together in the next tr, repeat from* till round. End with 4ch, sl st to the 3rd of 3ch.

Round 4   3ch (to count as 1tr), 2tr in next tr, 1tr in next tr, *4ch, miss 4ch, 1tr in tr, 2tr together in next tr, 1tr in next tr, repeat from* till the end of the round. End with 4ch, a sl st to the 3rd of 3ch at the beginning of the round.

Rounds 5 to 11   Continue to work as per diagram 1. Fasten off, sew in tail ends.

LINKING MOTIFS. These are joined by crocheting together as you complete the last full round. Join motifs in the order and position shown in diagram 1. The symbol ⟵ denotes the linking points.

TO MAKE A TABLE MAT (6 motifs). Begin by making one complete motif as above. Work a second motif, but leave the last full edge unworked and, while working on it, link motifs together using a sl st at the points shown on the diagram. Work to 7th dtr on the second last

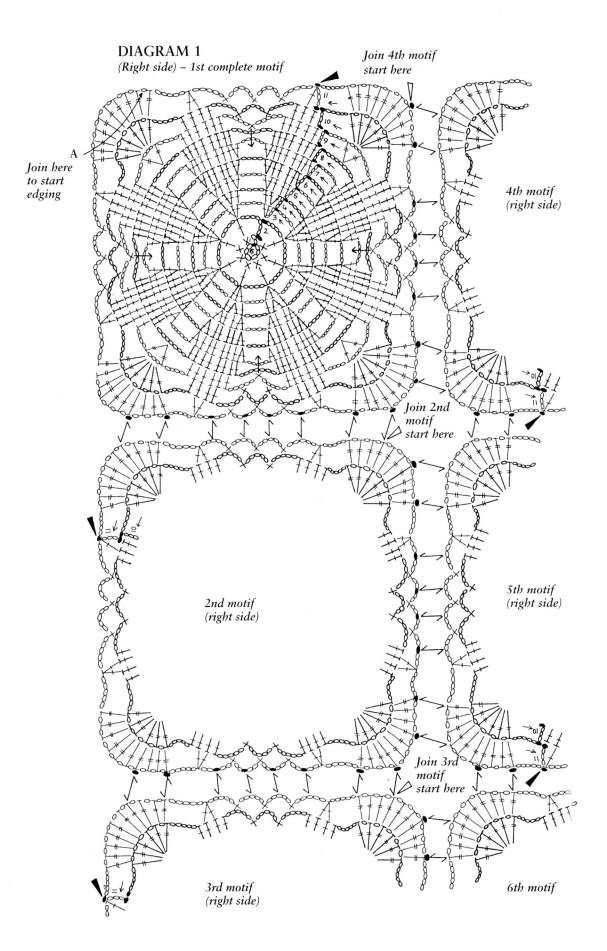

DIAGRAM 1
(Right side) – 1st complete motif

Join 4th motif start here

A
Join here to start edging

4th motif (right side)

Join 2nd motif start here

2nd motif (right side)

5th motif (right side)

Join 3rd motif start here

3rd motif (right side)

6th motif

corner group of sts, sl st across to the **first motif** (pushing the hook through the wrong side under the top 2 threads of dtr opposite). Complete the corner group of sts and, after the last dtr, work a sl st across to last dtr as before. Continue to complete the **second motif** and, at the same time, link across to the first motif, as shown on the diagram. Do not rush the process of linking the motifs. Fasten off.

Third motif – Join in the same way as second motif, starting at the point shown on diagram.

Fourth motif – Join to the right hand side of the first motif.

Fifth motif – Leave 2 full edges unworked and link as before to the fourth and second motifs.

Sixth motif – Work as fifth motif, but linking to the fifth and third motifs.

This completes the main section of the table mat.

EDGING FOR THE TABLE MAT

WORKING NOTES
◆ Before beginning the edge, **mark the centre 1ch sp** at each of the 4 corners with a safety pin, for future reference. Remove and replace as required.
◆ Refer to the diagram on page 23 throughout. Work all chs and dc firmly.

BEGIN. Join the thread to point **A**, in first 1ch space of the corner group (see diagram 2, opposite).

Round 1   3ch to count as first tr, 1tr in same sp, 2tr in each next 3 x 1ch sps, 3tr in next sp (marked space), 2tr in each next 4 x 1ch sps.This completes a corner group of 19tr. *5ch, 1dc in 5ch loop, repeat from* 5 more times, 5ch, 2tr in each next 5 x 1ch sps (10tr), miss the seam/join. 2tr in each of 5 x 1ch sps in the corner group of the next motif (check the

diagram), *5ch, dc in 5ch loop, repeat from* 5 more times, 5ch, 2tr in each next 5 x 1ch sps (10tr), miss seam/join, 2tr in each of 5 x 1ch sps in the corner group of the next motif. *5ch, 1dc in the next 5ch loop, repeat from* 5 times. 5ch, 2tr in each next 4 x 1ch sps, 3tr in the next sp (marked corner space), 2tr in each next 4 x 1ch sps. Continue to work the remaining 3 sides, following the diagram and **remembering** to work 3tr together in the centre of the marked sp at each corner. End with a sl st to the 3rd of 3ch at the beginning of the round.

Mark the first of 5ch on each of the following rounds to help identify the start and the finish of each round. Remove and replace the marker as you start each round.

Round 2   *5ch, miss 2trs, 1dc in next tr, repeat from* till 6 loops made, 5ch, miss 5ch loop, dc in next 5ch loop, *5ch, 1dc in next 5ch loop, repeat from* 3 more times, 5ch, miss 5ch loop, 1dc in tr, 5ch, miss 2tr, dc in next tr, 5ch, miss 2 tr, 1dc in next tr, 5ch, miss 6tr, 1dc in next tr, 5ch, miss 2tr, 1dc in next tr, 5ch, miss 2tr, 1dc in last tr, 5ch, miss 5ch loop, 1dc in loop, continue to work round all 4 sides as shown on the diagram. End with a sl st to first of the 5ch at the beginning of the round, sl st in each of the next 2ch.

Round 3   *5ch, 1dc in next 5ch loop, repeat from* on all 4 sides. End with a sl st to the first of 5ch at the beginning of the round, sl st in each of the next 2ch.

Round 4   *5ch, 1dc in the next loop, repeat from* as on round 3.

Round 5   5ch, 1dc in the next 5ch loop, **5tr in the next dc** (first corner), 1dc in the 5ch loop, *5ch, 1dc in next 5ch loop, repeat from* till 10 x 5ch loops from corner 5tr. 5tr in 5ch loop, 1dc in next loop, *5ch, 1dc in next loop, repeat from* till 9 x 5ch loops, 5tr in next 5ch loop, 1dc in next loop, work 10 more loops, **5tr in**

next dc (second corner), 1dc in next loop. First side is complete. Work 10 more loops, 5tr in next loop, 1dc in next loop, work 10 more loops, **5tr in next dc** (third corner), 1dc in next loop. Second side is complete. Work 10 more loops, 5tr in next loop, 1dc in next loop, work 9 loops, 5tr in next loop, 1dc in next loop, work 10 more loops, **5tr in next dc** (fourth corner), 1dc in next loop. Third side is complete. Finish the last side by working 10 more loops, 5tr in next loop, 1dc in next loop, work a further 9 loops until you reach the first 5ch loop at the beginning of the round, sl st to the first of 5ch to complete the round.

Round 6 sl st in each of next 2ch, work round the corner as follows: 5ch, 1dc in first tr of 5tr group, 5ch, miss 1tr, 1dc in next tr, 5ch, miss 1tr, 1dc in last tr, *5ch, 1dc in next loop, repeat from* 9 more times, 5ch, 1dc in the 3rd of 5tr group, *5ch, 1dc in next loop, repeat from*

8 more times, 5ch, 1dc in 3rd of 5tr group, 10 more loops, work round the corner as before – 5ch, 1dc in first tr of 5tr group, 5ch, miss 1tr, 1dc in the next tr, 5ch, miss 1tr, 1dc in the last tr. Continue round the remaining sides – taking care to place the dc accurately at the corners. End with a sl st to the first of 5ch at the beginning of the round.

Round 7 sl st in each next 2ch, *5ch, 1dc in next loop, repeat from* on all 4 sides. End with a sl st to the first of 5ch.

Round 8 As round 7. End with a sl st to first of 5ch, sl st in each next 2ch.

Round 9 3ch (to count as a tr), 1tr, 1htr, 1dc in first loop, 2ch, *(2tr, 1htr, 1dc, 2ch) in next loop, repeat from* on all 4 sides. End with a sl st to 3rd of 3ch. Fasten off, sew in all tail ends.

DIAGRAM 2
Edging for the table mat

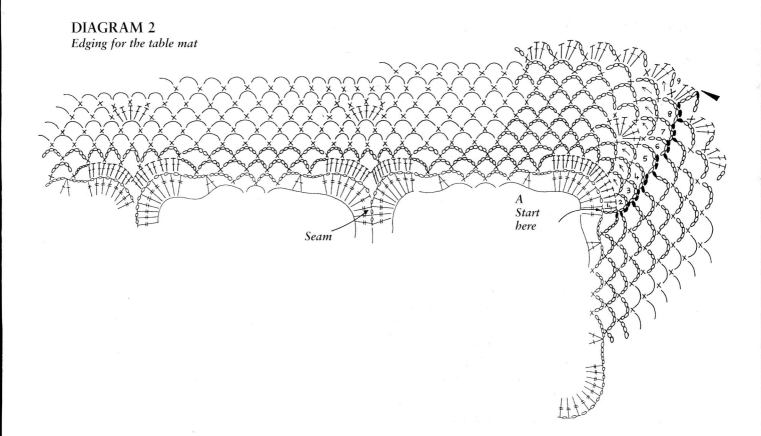

Seam

A
Start
here

MATCHING COASTER. Make 1 complete motif. Work edgings as follows (see diagram 3, opposite). Join the thread to point **A**, in the first 1ch sp of a corner group.

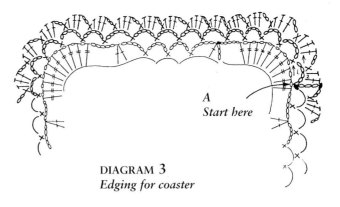

DIAGRAM 3
Edging for coaster

Round 1   *5ch, miss (1dtr, 1ch, 1dtr), 1dc in next 1ch sp, repeat from* 3 more times. *5ch, 1dc in next 5ch loop, repeat from* 5 times. 5ch, miss 1dtr, 1dc in first 1ch sp on next corner group, *5ch, miss (1dtr, 1ch, 1dtr), 1dc in the next 1ch sp, repeat from* 2 more times. Continue round the remaining sides following the diagram. End with a sl st to the first of 5ch.

Round 2   3ch (to count as a tr), (1tr, 1htr, 1dc) in first loop, 2ch, *(2tr, 1htr, 1dc, 2ch) in next loop, repeat from* on all 4 sides. End with a sl st to the 3rd of 3ch. Fasten off. Sew in tail ends.

The coaster – life-size

CUSHION (9 motifs)

Work the first 6 motifs as for the table mat. Link together. Work another 3 motifs and link to the previous ones (see diagram 4, opposite). Sew in the tail ends.

Once all the motifs are attached, press lightly on the wrong side with a damp cloth. Ease and pin into shape on a board covered with cling film. Leave to dry. There is no border around the cushion. A tassel, attached to a short chain (12ch) can be added to each of the 4 corners. Attach cotton to centre 1ch sp at corners and follow the instructions for the single ch tassel, below. Slip-stitch the completed crochet panel onto the centre of the cushion.

SINGLE CHAIN WITH TASSEL. Cut a length of cotton, at least 35 in / 89 cm. Thread through the suggested point on the pattern, under a double thread if possible, pull till the ends are of even length. In the same place, insert a slightly larger hook and work the required number of chains, using both tails together. Extend last ch loops. Remove the hook. Cut 12 short strands of cotton (8 in / 20 cm) and place evenly through the last ch loop. Pull loop tight. Fold strands in half and bind tightly 2 or 3 times, approximately ¼ in / 5 mm down from ch loop, using the remaining cotton tails. Thread tails through a darning needle and push the needle through the tassel, **once above** and **once below** the binding, in opposite directions. Finally go down through the binding, incorporating the tails into the tassel. Trim the ends.

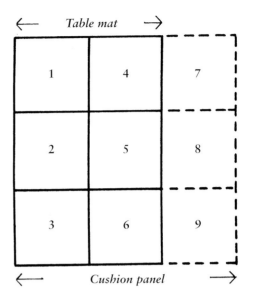

DIAGRAM 4
Sewing order for the table mat and for the cushion applique panel

ALTERNATIVE DOUBLE CHAIN. Cut a length of cotton 35 in / 89 cm approx. Thread through the suggested point on the pattern, under a double thread if possible. Pull till the cut ends are of even length. Tie a single knot close to the work. Insert the hook in the same place and pull one of the cotton threads through. Work required length of chs, and add the tassel as described above. Insert hook again and catch the remaining thread, working a second chain, the same length as the first. Add a tassel as before. Trim.

Opposite. Sugar starch bowl with a curved edge, see page 28.

SUGAR STARCH BOWL

Approximate sizes: Bowl with curved edge (page 27), diameter: 6½ in / 16.5 cm, depth: 2 in / 5 cm. Bowl with straight sides (see page 31), diameter: 5½ in / 14 cm, depth 2½ in / 6 cm

MATERIALS. Small quantity (less than 25 g), DMC Cébélia crochet cotton No 10 – pale yellow 745 or écru naturel, a 1.50 mm crochet hook

TENSION / GAUGE. The diameter of round 1 should measure ¾ in / 2 cm.

WORKING NOTES
◆ 3ch at beginning of each round count as 1tr.
◆ Change direction each round. **From round 11,** do not turn.
◆ If unsure where to place the sl st at the end of each round, **mark 3rd of 3ch** at beginning of round with a safety pin, removing and replacing it at the start of each round. Correct placing of sl st produces an almost invisible seam on the bowl.
◆ It is also important to have the correct number of stitches on each round and it is easier to count the stitches **before** you link them with a sl st. Adjust the number, if necessary, before continuing.
◆ For sugar starching, see method on page 30.
◆ Refer to stitch diagram opposite.

BEGIN. (See diagram on page 29.) 5ch, sl st to form a ring.

Round 1   3ch, 14tr into ring (15sts incl 3ch), sl st to 3rd of 3ch, turn.

Round 2   3ch, 1tr at the base of 3ch, *2tr together in each st, repeat from* till the end of the round (30sts incl 3ch), sl st to 3rd of 3ch, turn.

Round 3   3ch, 1tr at the base of 3ch, 1tr in next st, *2tr together in next st, 1tr in next st, repeat from* till the end of the round (45sts incl 3ch), sl st to 3rd of 3ch, turn.

Round 4   3ch, 1tr at the base of 3ch, *1tr in each next 2sts, 2tr together in next st, repeat from* till the end of the round. End with 1tr in each last 2sts (60sts incl 3ch), sl st to the 3rd of 3ch, turn.

Round 5   3ch, 1tr at the base of 3ch, *1tr in each next 3sts, 2tr together in next st, repeat from* till the end of the round. End with 1tr in each last 3sts (75sts incl 3ch), sl st to 3rd of 3ch, turn.

Round 6   3ch, 1tr in next st, **not** st at the base of 3ch, 1tr in each st till the end of the round (75sts incl 3ch) sl st to the 3rd of 3ch, turn.

Over the next few rounds, your work will begin to curve into a bowl shape.

Round 7   3ch, 1tr at the base of 3ch, *1tr in each next 5sts, 2tr together in next st, repeat from* till the end of the round. End with 1tr in each last 2sts, after last 2tr together (88 sts), sl st to the 3rd of 3ch, turn.

The sequence of sts will not work out exactly from round 7. Check diagram.

Round 8. 3ch, 1tr at base of 3ch, *1tr in each

DIAGRAM **1**

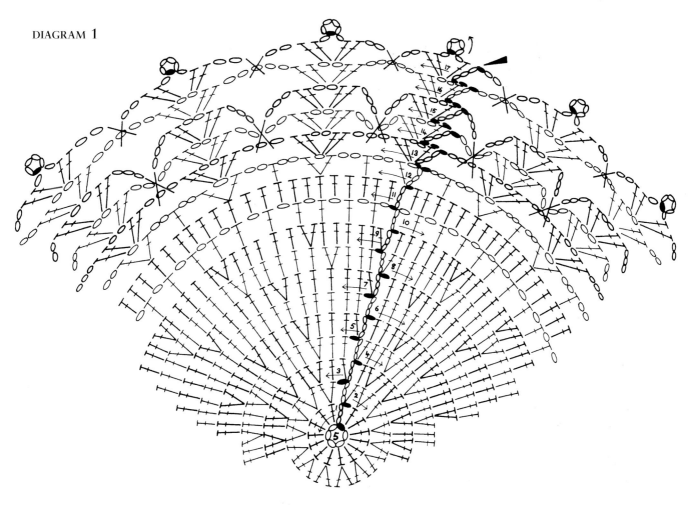

Right side

next 5sts, 2tr together in next st, repeat from* till the end of the round. End with 1tr in each last 3sts, after last 2tr together (103sts), sl st to the 3rd of 3ch, turn.

Round 9   3ch, 1tr at the base of 3ch, *1tr in each next 5sts, 2tr together in next st, repeat from* till the end of the round. End with 1tr in each last 6sts, after last 2tr together (120sts), sl st to the 3rd of 3ch, turn.

Round 10   4ch, miss st at the base of 4ch **and** next st, 1tr in next st, *1ch, miss a st, 1tr in next st, repeat from* till the end of the round. End with 1ch and a sl st to 3rd of 4ch (60sps), turn.

Round 11   3ch, 1tr in first sp, *1tr in next st,

1tr in next sp, repeat from* till the end of the round (120sts), sl st to the 3rd of 3ch.

From round 11   Do not turn. Work in the same direction till the pattern is complete. Check number of sts and adjust if necessary.

Round 12   4ch, 1tr at the base of 4ch, *2ch, miss 2sts, 1tr in the next st, 2ch, miss 2sts, (1tr, 1ch, 1tr) in next st, repeat from* till the end of the round. End with 2ch, miss 2sts, 1tr in the next st, 2ch, miss 2sts, sl st to the 3rd of 4ch, sl st **again** into 1ch sp.

Round 13   3ch, (1tr, 2ch, 2tr) in the first 1ch sp, *3ch, miss 2ch, 1tr, 2ch. Work (2tr, 2ch, 2tr) in next 1ch sp, repeat from* till the end of the round. End with 3ch, sl st to the 3rd of 3ch, sl st in the next tr **and again** into 1ch sp.

Round 14 3ch, (1tr, 2ch, 2tr) in the first 2ch sp *4ch, (2tr, 2ch, 2tr) in next 2ch sp, repeat from* till the end of the round. End with 4ch, sl st to the 3rd of 3ch, sl st in the next tr **and again** into 2ch sp.

Round 15 3ch, (1tr, 2ch, 2tr) in the first 2ch sp, *3ch, work a tight dc around 4ch on round 14 and 3ch on round 13, pulling the chains together (see diagram on page 29). 3ch, (2tr, 2ch, 2tr) in the next 2ch sp, repeat from* till the end of the round. End with 3ch, sl st to the 3rd of 3ch, sl st in the next tr **and again** in the 1ch sp.

Round 16 3ch, (1tr, 2ch, 2tr) in first 2ch sp, *5ch, (2tr, 2ch, 2tr) in next 2ch sp, repeat from* till round. End with 5ch, and a sl st to the 3rd of 3ch, sl st in next tr **and again** in the 1ch sp.

Round 17 3ch, 1tr in 2ch sp, (1ch, 1 x 4ch picot, 1ch, 2tr) in same 2ch sp, *2ch, 1 tight dc around 5ch on round 16, 2ch, (2tr, 1ch, 1 x 4ch picot, 1ch, 2tr) in next 2ch sp, repeat from* till the end of the round. End with 2ch, 1 tight dc around 5ch, 2ch, sl st to the 3rd of 3ch. Fasten off, sew in tail ends.

SUGAR STARCHING

Use this traditional method to stiffen a piece of work so that it can be used as a free-standing object, such as the bowls featured here. The same method can be used to starch small suitable motifs to produce the components of a mobile or to make Christmas tree decorations.

MATERIALS. Half a cup of granulated sugar, half a cup of water, a plain glass bowl to use as a mould for the crochet shape (up to 6 in / 15 cm in diameter). A large plate or tray on which to stand the glass bowl while the crochet is wet.

METHOD. Mix sugar and water in a small pan, place over a low heat. Stir till sugar is completely dissolved, using a wooden spoon. Do not allow to boil. Remove from heat and allow to cool. Soak the piece of crochet thoroughly in the sugar solution and squeeze out the excess liquid gently.

STRAIGHT-SIDED BOWL (see opposite)
Turn glass bowl upside down and carefully fit the lace over the bowl. Centre the base of the work as accurately as you can. Smooth the sides of the work over the bowl and gently pull out the picots, to the same length and spacing all round. Allow to dry for at least 24 hours. Then ease a palette knife between the glass bowl and the crochet but do not remove. Allow to dry for at least another 12 hours. Carefully remove the work from its glass mould.

BOWL WITH CURVED EDGE (see page 27)
Starch as explained above. After a few hours, and when the crochet begins to stiffen, gently bend the last two rows of crochet outward, as evenly as possible. Before the work hardens fully, check that you are fully satisfied with the edge and adjust it if necessary. Once completely dry, sew or glue tiny pearls at the tip of each point. In a damp atmosphere, the starched object can become sticky. To prevent this, spray the finished article with a studio preservative spray. If dirty, wash the object in plenty of warm soapy water, rinsing it well in clear water. Dry fully and starch again.

SQUARE PIN CUSHION

Approximate size: 3 in / 7.5 cm square

MATERIALS. 25g DMC Cébélia crochet cotton No 10 – pale yellow 745 or white 5200, a 1.50 mm crochet hook, a scrap of silk or cotton fabric to cover the cushion pad, a small amount of polyester wadding

TENSION / GAUGE

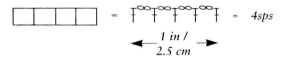

= 4sps

1 in / 2.5 cm

WORKING NOTES

◆ The panel consists entirely of open mesh filet, with 2 ch between the trs.

BEGIN. 41ch (see diagram 1).

DIAGRAM 1

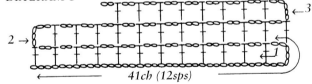

41ch (12sps)

Row 1   1tr in 8th ch from hook, *work 2ch, miss 2ch, 1tr in next ch, repeat from* to the end of the row (12 x 2ch sps), 5ch, turn.

Row 2   Miss 2ch, 1tr in next tr, *2ch, miss 2ch, 1tr in next tr, repeat from* to the end of the row. Finish with 2ch, miss 2ch, 1tr in next ch, 5ch, turn.

Row 3   As row 2. Repeat till 13 rows from the start. Do not turn, do not cut the thread.

DECREASING EDGE

Round 1   2ch, 2dc in the corner sp, 2dc in each of the following ch sps, 5dc in corner sp, continue in the same way until you reach the starting corner sp, 2dc in this sp, sl st to 2ch to complete the round. Do not cut the thread, hold the loop with a safety pin.

At this stage, you should make the inner cloth cover for the pad. Cut 2 pieces of fabric, ½ in / 1.5 cm bigger than the crochet square to allow for the seams. With right sides together, stitch around, leaving an opening along the fourth side. Turn out and fill with wadding, pushing it well into the corners. Close the opening.

This pattern can also be used to produce a lavender sachet. Proceed exactly as described, but replace the wadding with lavender or pot pourri (see page 49), where such a square sachet is shown, together with a round one). These small projects are quick and easy to work, yet make delightful presents.

DECREASING EDGE (continued)

Having completed the inner pad cover, you can resume the work to form the back of the crochet cover. Remove the safety pin from the corner of the crochet panel and work 3ch. The next 4 rounds must be worked very firmly.

Round 2   1tr in each dc on all 4 sides of the mesh square. The work should now begin to curve inwards to form a casing for the cushion pad. End with a sl st to 3rd of 3ch at the beginning of the round, 3ch, turn.

Round 3   Decrease next 2tr, *1tr in each next 2sts, decrease next 2tr, repeat from*. End with a sl st to the 3ch at beginning of the round, 3ch, turn.

Round 4   Decrease next 2tr, *1tr in each next 3sts, decrease 2tr, repeat from*. End with a sl st to the 3ch at the beginning of the round, 3ch, turn.

Round 5   1tr in each stitch till the end of the round. By now, the edge of the work should be sufficiently curved to achieve a snug fit on the cushion pad. If not, repeat round 5, decreasing 2tr every 8th or 10th st till the end of the round, sl st to the 3rd of 3ch at the beginning of the round. Fasten off. Sew in tail ends.

PICOT EDGING

With the right side of the work facing you, join the thread by tying it once around the stem/post (see diagram 2) of a corner tr, on the last row of the mesh panel, 3ch, *1dc around stem/post of

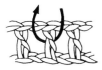

DIAGRAM 2
stem or post - (the vertical part of the stitch)

the next tr, 3ch, repeat from* working 3ch at the corners till the end of the round. End with a sl st to the first of 3ch at the beginning of the round. **Do not turn.** 2ch (to count as 1dc), (1dc, 1 x 4ch picot, 1dc) in the first 3ch loop and in each 3ch loop until the round is complete. End with a sl st to the 2nd of 2ch at the beginning of the round, work 25ch (firmly), sl st to base of 25ch. Turn and work 30dc in 25ch loop, sl st to first dc. This completes the loop from which to hang the pin cushion. Fasten off. Sew in tail ends. Ease the cover over the prepared pad.

Below: This romantic square pin cushion is based on a popular Victorian design, which forms part of the collection shown on page 33.

VICTORIAN PIN CUSHION

Approximate size, including frill: 5¼ x 6 in / 13.5 x 15 cm

MATERIALS. 25g DMC Cébélia crochet cotton No 10 - white 5200, a 1.50 mm crochet hook, a scrap of silk or cotton fabric to cover the pad, a small amount of polyester wadding, 36 in / 1 m of narrow ribbon

STITCHES, ABBREVIATIONS & SYMBOLS

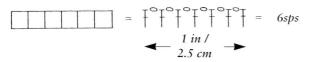

TENSION / GAUGE

WORKING NOTES

♦ 1ch between trs on open mesh
♦ Refer to the diagram opposite.

BEGIN. 46ch.

Row 1 1tr in 6th ch from hook, *1ch, miss 1ch, 1tr in next ch, repeat from* to the end. End with 1tr in last ch st (21sps), 4ch, turn.

Row 2 Miss 1ch, 1tr in tr, *1ch, miss 1ch, 1tr in tr, repeat from* till 6sps made. Work 1tr in sp, 1tr in tr (last 3trs make 1 block), (see diagram 1). Continue, following the diagram and working the blocks and spaces to complete the star design (21 rows). **Do not fasten off.** 2ch, work 2dc (firmly) into every 1ch sp around the edge

of the filet pattern, adding an extra 2dc in the corner sps. End with a sl st to the 2nd of 2ch. **Do not fasten off.** Hold the loop with a safety pin.

At this stage, cut 2 pieces of fabric, ½ in / 1.5 cm larger all round than the crochet panel to allow for the seams. Stitch the 2 pieces, right sides together, leaving a gap along one side to turn

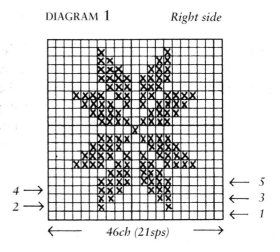

DIAGRAM **1**   *Right side*

46ch (21sps)

the work. Turn out, fill with wadding till quite firm, making sure it goes right into the corners. Slip-stitch the opening.

TO COMPLETE THE CROCHET COVER

Remove the safety pin from the working loop (see diagram 2, on page 36).

Round 1 3ch, dec 2tr, *1tr in next st, dec 2tr, rep from* till round all 4 sides, a sl st to the 3rd of 3ch to complete the round. 3ch, do not turn.

DIAGRAM 2

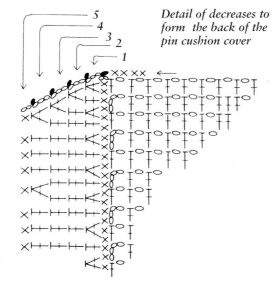

Detail of decreases to form the back of the pin cushion cover

Round 2   Decrease next 2tr, *1tr in each st till you reach the next corner, decrease 3tr at corner, repeat from* till round. End with a sl st to the 3rd of 3ch, 3ch, do not turn. The mesh panel should now begin to curve inwards to form a casing, if not, check the tension and if necessary rework round 2, using a smaller hook. Then continue as follows:

Round 3   As round 2, but decrease 2tr at the corners. End with a sl st to the 3rd of 3ch, 3ch, do not turn.

Check the fit again. **If too loose**, repeat round 2, decrease 2tr at the corners **and** decrease 2 or 3tr together at the centre of each side. Check the fit once again, then continue:

Round 4   Decrease next 2tr, *1tr in each of next 3sts, dec 2tr, repeat from* till the end of the round, sl st to the 3rd of 3ch, 2ch, do not turn.

Round 5   1dc in each st, work firmly to obtain a firm edge. This last round can be repeated if the cover is still a little loose. Fasten off. Sew in tail ends.

FRILL

Join the thread by tying it around the stem or post of a tr, at one of the corners of the front panel (see diagram 3). *3ch, 1dc around stem of next tr, repeat from* till you reach the **first** 3ch loop, 1dc in that loop, *5ch, 1dc in next 3ch loop, repeat from* till you reach the **first** 5ch loop, 1dc in that loop. *7ch, 1dc in next 5ch loop, repeat from* till you reach the **first** 7ch loop, 1dc in that loop. If you wish to have a fuller frill, add another round of 7ch loops. Cut the thread and fasten off. Sew in tail ends.

DIAGRAM 3
Stem or post (the vertical part of the stitch)

TO COMPLETE

Cut the ribbon into 2 equal lengths. Start threading it at one corner, on the last round of the main panel, just before the first round of the frill. Continue threading the ribbon over and under the stem or post of trs, until half way round, finishing at one corner. Thread the other length of ribbon through the remaining 2 edges. Even up tail ends, tie in small neat bows in the 2 corners, trim.

IRISH ROSE PIN CUSHION

Approximate size (including the frill): 4½ in / 12 cm in diameter

MATERIALS. 25g DMC Cébélia crochet cotton No 10 – white 5200 – or oddments, a 1.50 mm crochet hook, a scrap of silk or cotton fabric to cover the pad, a small amount of polyester wadding

WORKING NOTES
- Refer to the diagrams on page 38.
- Note the special ending on rounds 2 to 7.
- It may help to mark the first ch loop of each round. Remove and replace the marker as you work.

BEGIN. 7ch, sl st to form a ring (see diagram 1).

Round 1   1ch, 12dc in ring, sl st to first dc. **Do not turn** on this or any of the following rounds.

Round 2   3ch, miss 1dc, 1dc in next st *3ch, 1dc in the next dc, repeat from*. End with 1ch, 1htr in the first dc.

Round 3   4ch, 1dc in 3ch sp, *4ch, 1dc in the next 3ch sp, repeat from*. End with 1ch, 1tr in htr of previous round.

Round 4   *5ch, 1dc in 4ch sp, repeat from*. End with 2ch, 1tr in tr of previous round. Continue, following diagram 1, until you **complete round 9**. **Take note** of the number of ch sts and of the stitch used to complete each round.

Round 9   Should have 66 x 1ch sps (adjust to correct number of sps, if necessary). Do not

fasten off. Hold the loop with a safety pin.

At this stage, cut 2 pieces of material ½ in / 1.5 cm larger all round than the crochet panel. Stitch together, right sides facing, leaving a gap to insert the pad. Turn out. Fill with wadding, pushing it well into the corners. Close the opening.

TO COMPLETE THE BACK OF THE COVER
Remove the safety pin and decrease as follows:

Round 10   2ch, (1htr, 1ch in each 1ch sp) till the end of the round, sl st to 2ch. **Do not turn.**

Round 11   2ch, 1htr in first htr, *miss 1ch, 1htr in next htr, repeat from* till the end of the round, sl st to 2ch.

Round 12   2ch, 1htr in each next 4sts, *decrease 2htr, 1htr in each next 4sts, repeat from* till the end of the round, sl st to 2ch. (The sequence of sts may not work out exactly on this round.)

Round 13   2ch, 1htr in each st (work firmly), sl st to 2ch. Try the cover on the pad. **If it is a little loose, add an extra round of tightly worked dc.** Fasten off. Sew in tail ends.

DECORATIVE FRILL
Round 1   Tie thread around the stem or post of any tr on round 9 (see diagram 2). Work 4ch, *1dc around stem of next tr, 4ch, repeat from* till the end of the round. End with 4ch and a sl st to the first of 4ch at the beginning of the round.

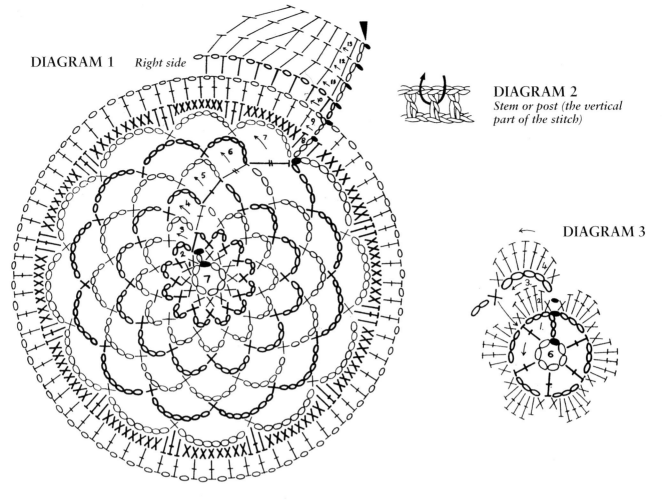

DIAGRAM 1 *Right side*

DIAGRAM 2
Stem or post (the vertical part of the stitch)

DIAGRAM 3

Round 2 sl st in next ch st, 5ch, *1dc in next 4ch sp, 5ch, repeat from*. End with 5ch, and a sl st to the first of 5ch at the beginning of the round.

Round 3 sl st in each next 2ch sts, 5ch, 1dc in first 5ch sp, *(5ch, 1dc, 5ch, 1dc) in next 5ch sp, repeat from* till the end of round. End with 5ch, sl st to first of 5ch at the beginning of the round. Fasten off. Sew in tail ends.

IRISH ROSE MOTIF (see diagram 3)

BEGIN. 6ch, sl st to form a ring,

Round 1 6ch, 1tr in ring, *3ch, 1tr in ring, repeat from* till the 5th sp. End with 3ch, sl st to 3rd of 6ch, making 6sps altogether. Do not turn.

Round 2 (1dc, 1htr, 3tr, 1htr, 1dc) in first 3ch sp, and in each 3ch sp till the end of the round, sl st to the first dc (6 petals). Do not turn.

Round 3 Work 5ch behind first petal, 1dc in tr on round 1 (between 2dcs), *5ch behind the next petal, 1dc in next tr, repeat from* till 6 x 5ch loops, sl st to first of 5ch at beginning of the round. Do not turn.

Round 4 (1dc, 1htr, 5tr, 1htr, 1dc) in each of 6 loops, sl st to dc at the beginning of the round. Fasten off. Sew in tail ends.

Attach the rose to the centre of the prepared cover. Slip it over the pad. Your Irish rose pin cushion is now ready.

To make a smaller version of the rose pin cushion, or to produce covers for guest soaps, as shown on this page, use DMC crochet cotton No 20, with a 1.25 mm crochet hook.

TEA TRAY CLOTH

Approximate size: 18 x 12 in / 46 x 30.5 cm

MATERIALS. 100 g DMC Cébélia crochet cotton No 10 – white 5200, a 1.50 mm crochet hook

STITCHES, ABBREVIATIONS & SYMBOLS

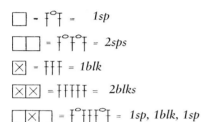

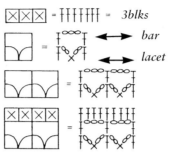

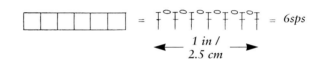

TENSION / GAUGE

DIAGRAM 1   *Right side*   *For instructions on finishing the edge, see diagram 2, page 42*

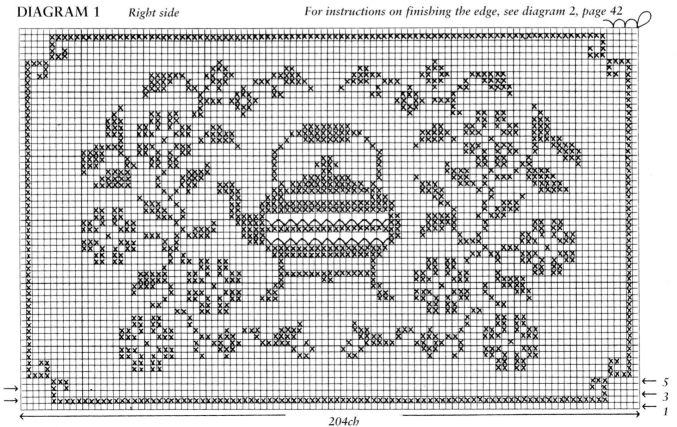

204ch
(100sps)

WORKING NOTES

♦ 1ch between trs on open mesh
♦ You may may find it useful to colour in each row on a photocopy of the diagram, as the work proceeds.

BEGIN. 204ch.

Row 1 1tr in 6th ch from hook, *1ch, miss 1ch, 1tr in next ch, repeat from* to the end (100sps), 4ch, **turn.**

Row 2 Miss 1ch, 1tr in next tr, *1ch, miss 1ch, 1tr in next tr, repeat from* till 5sps made, 1tr in next sp, 1tr in next tr (1 block). Continue this row as shown on diagram 1. End with 5sps, 4ch, **turn.**

Continue, following diagram 1, working blocks and spaces to a firm even tension, till you reach row 60 (top right hand-corner of panel). **Do not fasten off.**

FINISHED EDGE (see diagram 2)
With the right side of the work facing you, work 8ch (tightly), 1 dc into st at the base of the 8ch (1 corner loop made). *Work 5ch, miss 2sps,

1dc in next tr, repeat from* till you reach the next corner, work 8ch, 1dc beside last dc of 2nd corner loop is made). *Work 5ch, miss 2sps, 1dc in tr (opposite the end of the row). Repeat from* till the next corner point, work 8ch, 1dc beside last dc. *Work 5ch, miss 2sps, 1dc in next tr, repeat from* along lower edge. Continue till you have worked all 4 edges. End with a sl st at the base of the first 8ch loop. **Do not turn,** continue in the same direction, working firmly. *7dc in 8ch loop, 4dc in each 5ch loop till you reach next 8ch loop, repeat from* on all 4 sides. End with a sl st to first dc at the beginning of the round. Fasten off, sew in all tail ends.

TO COMPLETE
Press lightly on the wrong side, using a damp cloth. Ease gently into shape. If necessary, pin on a board covered with cling film and allow to dry fully.

Detail of finished edge

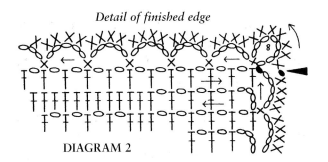

DIAGRAM 2

LACY JEWELLERY CUSHION

Approximate size of panel: 5 in / 13 cm square

MATERIALS. Oddment of DMC Cébélia crochet cotton No 10 – white 5200, a 1.50 mm crochet hook, a 8 in / 20 cm square cushion pad, 20 in / 50 cm of raw silk or other fabric for the cover

SPECIAL STITCHES (see page 13)

 = *5 loop puff st*

 = *double puff st group*

TENSION / GAUGE
The diameter of rounds 1 and 2 should measure 1¼ in / 3 cm.

WORKING NOTES
◆ Work to a firm, even tension and refer to the diagram on page 45 throughout.

BEGIN. 8ch, sl st to form a ring.

Round 1 3ch (to count as a tr), 2tr in ring, 4 ch, *3tr in ring, 4ch, repeat from* 2 more times, sl st to 3rd of 3ch. **Do not turn on this or any of the following rounds.**

Round 2 3ch, 1tr in each next 2trs, *(3tr, 3ch, 3tr) in corner sp, 1tr in each next 3tr, repeat from* 2 more times. End with (3tr, 3ch, 3tr) in last corner sp. Sl st to 3rd of 3ch, sl st again into next tr.

Round 3 3ch (to count as 1tr), 6tr at the base of 3ch, making a 7tr group. *3ch, 1 double puff st group in the corner loop, 3ch, miss 4tr, 7tr in next tr, miss 4tr, repeat from* 2 more times. End with 3ch, 1 double puff st group in the last corner, 3ch, sl st to 3rd of 3ch.

Round 4 6ch (to count as 1dtr and 2ch), 1dtr in next tr, *2ch, 1 dtr in next tr, repeat from* 4 more times (6 x 2ch sps between dtrs), 3ch, miss 3ch, 1 double puff st group in the next 2ch corner sp, 3ch, miss 3ch, 1dtr in first tr, *2ch, 1dtr in next tr, repeat from* 5 more times, 3ch, miss 3ch, 1 double puff st group in the next 2ch corner sp. Repeat st sequence, 2 more times (see diagram on page 45). End with a sl st to the 4th of 6ch, sl st again in the next ch st.

Note: Mark the first of the 4ch from the 5th round onwards as a guide to the beginning and the end of each round. Remove and replace the marker as you work.

Round 5 *4ch, 1dc in next 2ch sp, repeat from* 4 more times (5 loops), 5ch, miss 3ch, 1 double puff st group in next 2ch corner sp, 5ch, miss 3ch, 1dc in next 2ch sp. Repeat st sequence till the end of the round. End with 5ch, sl st to the first of 4ch (marked, see above). Sl st again in the next ch st.

Round 6 *4ch, 1dc in next 4ch loop, repeat from* 3 more times (4 loops), 7ch, miss 5ch, 1 double puff st group in 2ch corner sp, 7ch, miss 5ch, 1dc in next 4ch loop. Repeat st sequence till the end of the round. End with 7ch, sl st to

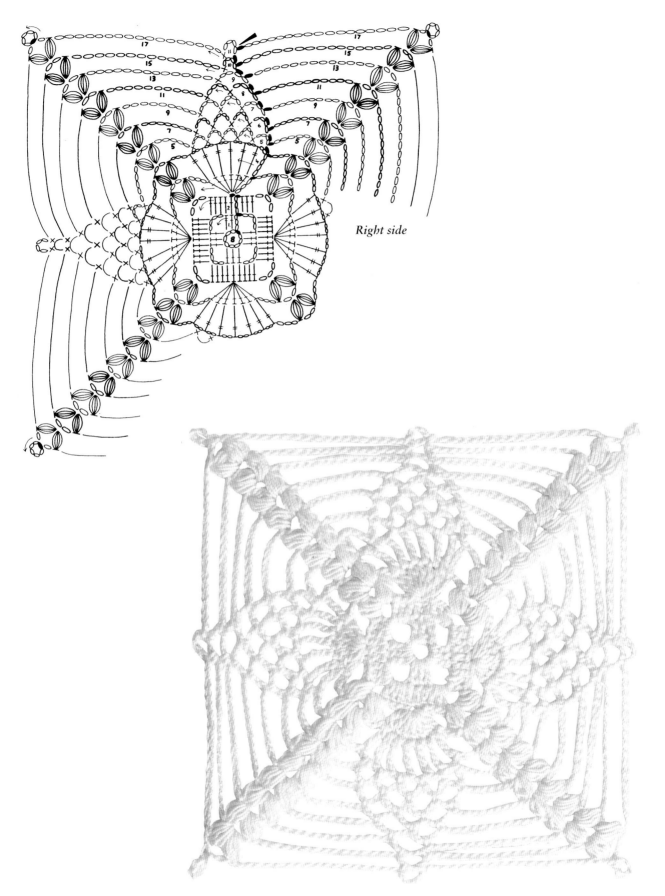

Right side

The crochet motif, shown life-size.

first of 4ch (marked), sl st again in the next ch st.

Round 7   *4ch, 1dc in next 4ch loop, rep from* 2 more times (3 loops), 9ch, miss 7ch, 1 double puff st group in the 2ch corner sp, 9ch, miss 7ch, 1dc in next 4ch loop. Repeat the st sequence till the end of the round. End with 9ch, sl st to the first of 4ch (marked). Sl st again in next ch st.

Round 8   4ch, 1dc in next loop, 4ch, 1dc in next loop (2 loops), 11ch, miss 9ch, 1 double puff st group in the 2ch corner sp, 11ch, miss 9ch, 1dc in next 4ch loop. Repeat the st sequence till the end of the round. End with 11ch, sl st to the first of 4ch, sl st again in the next ch st.

Round 9   4ch, 1dc in next loop, *13ch, miss 11ch, 1 double puff st group in 2ch corner sp, 13ch, miss 11ch, 1dc in next 4ch loop, 4ch, 1dc in next 4ch loop. Repeat the st sequence from* till the end of the round. End with 13ch, sl st to first of 4ch. Sl st again in the next ch st.

Round 10   4ch, 1dc back in same loop, *15ch, miss 13ch, 1 double puff st group in 2ch corner sp, 15ch, miss 13ch, (1dc, 4ch, 1dc) in 4ch loop. Repeat the st sequence from* till the end of the round. End with 15ch, sl st to first of 4ch. Sl st again in the next ch st.

Round 11   4ch, 1dc back in same loop, 17ch, miss 15ch, *(1 x 5 loop puff st, 1ch, 1 x 5ch picot, 1ch, 1 x 5 loop puff st) in 2ch corner sp, 17ch, miss 15ch, (1dc, 4ch, 1dc) in next 4ch loop, 17ch, miss 15ch, repeat the st sequence from*. End with 17ch after the last corner and sl st to first of 4ch. Fasten off, sew in tail ends.

TO COMPLETE

Press lightly on the wrong side of the work, using a damp cloth. Ease into shape by pulling gently at the corners. Pin out evenly on a flat board covered in cling film. Open out the picots. Leave to dry. Attach the motif in the centre of the jewellery cushion with a few stitches or with pearl-headed pins, as shown in the photograph on page 44. This makes it easier to remove the lace panel and wash it.

MAKING UP THE CUSHION

Cut 2 pieces of silk, or other fabric, measuring 7½ in / 19.5 cm square (this includes a ½ in / 1.5 cm seam allowance all round). For the frill, cut a strip 3¼ in / 8 cm wide. To save fabric, several strips can be cut and joined to obtain a total length of 72 in / 1.90 m. Join the 2 ends of the frill to form a ring. Press and open out the seams. Right side uppermost, fold the strip in half, lengthwise, and press flat. Gather the edge to fit around the perimeter of the cushion. Pin the frill around one of the fabric squares and machine-stitch. Put the work down on the table with the frill uppermost. Pin the second square of fabric on top of it and machine-stitch, leaving a 3½ in / 9 cm gap in the centre of one of the sides to turn the work. Press. Fit the pad inside the cover and slip-stitch the opening.

LAVENDER SACHET

Approximate diameter: 5 in / 13 cm

MATERIALS. 25 g DMC Cébélia crochet cotton No 10 – pale yellow 745, a 1.50 mm crochet hook, a handful of lavender, a scrap of lightweight fabric for the inner pouch, 20 in / 50 cm of narrow ribbon

WORKING NOTES
♦ Always work in the same direction, firmly and evenly, and refer to the stitch diagram on page 48 throughout.

FRONT OF THE SACHET

BEGIN. 6ch, sl st to form a ring.

Round 1 5ch (to count as 1tr and 2ch), (1tr, 2ch in ring) 7 times, sl st to the 3rd of 5ch (8 x 2ch sps).

Round 2 sl st again in first 2ch sp, 3ch, 2tr in sp beside 3ch, 2ch, *3tr in next 2ch sp, 2ch, repeat from* in each 2ch sp till the end of the round. End with a sl st to 3rd of 3ch at the beginning of the round (8 x 3tr groups and 8 x 2ch sps).

Round 3 3ch, 1tr at base of 3ch, 1tr in next tr, 2tr together in last tr of 3tr group, 2ch, miss 2ch, *2tr together in next tr, 1tr in next tr, 2tr together in last tr of 3tr group, 2ch, miss 2ch, repeat from* till the end of the round. End with a sl st to the 3rd of 3ch.

Round 4 3ch (to count as first tr), 1tr in each next 4tr, 2ch, 1tr in 2ch sp, 2ch, *1tr in each next 5tr, 2ch, 1tr in 2ch sp, 2ch, repeat from* till the end of the round, sl st to 3rd of 3ch.

Round 5 3ch, 1tr in next tr, decrease next 2tr, 1tr in next tr, 2ch, 1tr in 2ch sp, 2ch, 1tr in tr, 2ch, 1tr in next sp, 2ch, *1tr in each next 2tr, dec next 2tr, 1tr in next tr, 2ch, 1tr in 2ch sp, 1tr in tr, 2ch, 1tr in next sp, 2ch, repeat from* till the end of the round, sl st to the 3rd of 3ch.

Round 6 3ch, decrease next 2tr, 1tr in next tr, (2ch, 1tr in 2ch sp) 4 times, 2ch, *1tr in next tr, decrease next 2tr, 1tr in next tr, (2ch, 1tr in 2ch sp) 4 times, 2ch, repeat from* till the end of the round, sl st to 3rd of 3ch.

Round 7 sl st again in next st, 5ch, miss 1tr, *(1tr in 2ch sp, 2ch) in each next 5sps, 2ch, miss 1tr, 1tr in next st, miss 1tr, 2ch, repeat from* till the end of the round, sl st to the 3rd of 5ch (48 sps).

Round 8 Work this round slightly tighter. 1ch, *3dc in next 2ch sp, repeat from* till the end of the round, sl st to the first dc at the beginning of the round.

Round 9 5ch, miss 1 st, 1tr in next st, 2ch, *miss 1 st, 1tr in next st, repeat from* till the end of the round, sl st to the 3rd of 5ch (72 sps). It is important to have the correct number of spaces on this round.

Round 10 sl st again in the first 2ch sp, 5ch, 1tr in same sp as 5ch, 1ch, 1dc in next 2ch sp, 1ch, *(1tr, 2ch, 1tr) in next 2ch sp, 1ch, 1dc in next 2ch sp, 1ch, repeat from* till the end of the round, sl st to 3rd of 5ch.

Round 11 sl st again in first ch sp, 3ch, (3tr, 1 x 4ch picot, 4tr) in same sp as 3ch, 1dc in next 2ch sp, *(4tr, 1 x 4ch picot, 4tr) in next 2ch sp, 1dc in next 2ch sp, repeat from* till the end of the round, sl st to the 3rd of 3ch. Fasten off, sew in tail ends.

BACK OF THE SACHET
Proceed exactly as for the front panel, but omit rounds 10 and 11.

INNER POUCH
Cut 2 circles of fabric, ½ in / 1.5 cm larger than the back section of the sachet. Sew the pieces together, leaving a small opening to turn the work. Fill the pouch with lavender (do not overfill). Close the opening with a few slip stitches.

ASSEMBLING THE SACHET
Overlap the 2 pieces of crochet, wrong sides together, and carefully thread the narrow ribbon in and out of round 9 to join the 2 layers. Leave a gap through which to insert the lavender bag. When this is done, continue weaving the ribbon. Tie a neat bow on the front of the sachet.

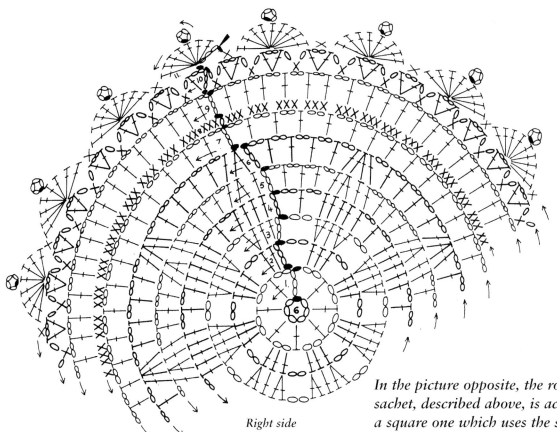

Right side

In the picture opposite, the round lavender sachet, described above, is accompanied by a square one which uses the same pattern as the pin cushion on page 32.

LUCKY STAR CUSHION

Approximate size of the cushion (excluding the frill): 12 in / 30.5 cm square

MATERIALS. 100 g DMC Cébélia crochet cotton No 10 – white 5200, a 1.50 mm crochet hook, 1 cushion pad 13 in / 33 cm square, white or contrasting silk or other fabric to cover the cushion pad, 110 in / 3 m narrow ribbon, decorative bow (optional)

STITCHES, ABBREVIATIONS & SYMBOLS

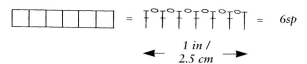

TENSION / GAUGE

CHECKING THE TENSION
The length of the first row should be no less than 12 in / 30.5 cm and no more than 13 in / 33 cm. If too tight, use a bigger hook, if too loose, use a smaller hook.

WORKING NOTES
♦ 1ch between trs on open mesh
♦ Make a photocopy of the diagram on page 52.

BEGIN. 135ch, fairly tight and even.

Row 1   1tr in 6th ch from hook. *1ch, miss 1ch, 1tr in next ch, repeat from* to the end of the row (65sps), 4ch, **turn**. Check the tension and the length of the first row before continuing.

Row 2   Miss 1ch sp, 1tr in tr, *1ch, miss ch sp, 1tr in tr, repeat from* to end, 4ch, **turn**.

Row 3   as row 2

Now follow the diagram, working blocks and spaces to form the motif until you reach the half-way point, then turn the prepared photocopy upside down and proceed with the second half of the design (65 rows). **Do not fasten off.**

DECORATIVE FRILL (front panel only)
5ch, 1dc in first sp, mark this first loop with a safety pin, 5ch, 1dc in next sp, work all around the edge of the panel, working an extra loop in corner sps, till you reach the marked loop. *Remove marker pin. Work 5ch, 1dc in that loop, replace the pin in the completed loop and continue, working 5ch, 1dc in the next loop, till you reach the marked loop. Repeat from* till 7 rounds are complete. Fasten off, sew in all tail ends. For a fuller frill, add 1 or 2 extra rounds.

TO COMPLETE THE COVER
The star design can be repeated on the back of the cushion, or substituted by a plain filet crochet mesh: 1tr, 1ch, 1tr worked over the 135ch (65sps) and for 65 rows. Fasten off, sew in all tail ends. Press both sections lightly, using a damp cloth, ease into shape. Pin out to correct size if necessary.

Right side

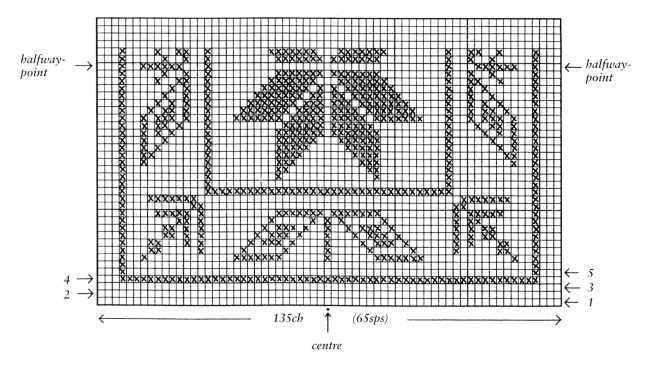

halfway-point →

← *halfway-point*

4 →
2 →

← 5
← 3
← 1

←————————— 135ch ↑ (65sps) —————————→

centre

ASSEMBLING THE CUSHION

Make up the fabric cover by cutting 2 squares of the selected fabric, allowing ½ in / 1.5 cm for the seams. Machine-stitch, leaving a 6 in / 15 cm gap to turn out the work. Insert pad and slip-stitch the gap.

Overlay the 2 filet crochet panels, wrong sides together, ensuring that the spaces in the filet are aligned. Cut the ribbon in half and thread one length through the outer edges of the first 2 sides, threading it over and under trs. Start at a corner space (just before the onset of the frill). Thread the remaining ribbon through the third side and slip the prepared cushion inside the cover before threading the ribbon through the fourth side. Even out the 2 ends of the ribbon and tie in neat bows. Alternatively, a bow made with a wider ribbon can be fixed with a couple of stitches at one corner.

DAINTY BOOKMARKS

STRAIGHT BOOKMARK (see diagram opposite)

Approximate length, including tassel: 8 in / 20 cm

MATERIALS. Oddments of DMC Cébélia crochet cotton No 10 – white 5200, pale blue 800, pale yellow 745, a 1.50 mm crochet hook

BEGIN. 6ch, sl st to form a ring.

Row 1 3ch (to count as a tr), (2tr, 3ch, 3tr) in ring, **not** in ch sts, 3ch, **turn.**

Row 2 Miss 2tr, (3tr, 3ch, 3tr) in 3ch sp, miss 2tr, 1tr in 3rd of 3ch on row before, 3ch, **turn.**

Row 3 Miss 3tr, (3tr, 3ch, 3tr) in 3ch sp, miss 3tr, 1tr in 3rd of 3ch on row before, 3ch, **turn.**

Row 4 to row 12 Work as row 3.

Row 13 Work as row 3 but omit the final 3ch, turn at the end of the row. **Do not fasten off.**

Row 14 (Edging) 2ch, following the diagram opposite, work along the 1st long side of the bookmark, 3dc in first sp, 3dc in next sp till you reach the end of the top edge. End with 1 sl st to the 2nd of 2ch at the start of edging. Fasten off, sew in tail ends. Complete by adding a tassel at the end of 12ch or the alternative double ch with tassels. The instructions for tassel making are on page 26.

Note: A decorative edge worked in a contrasting colour can be added if desired.

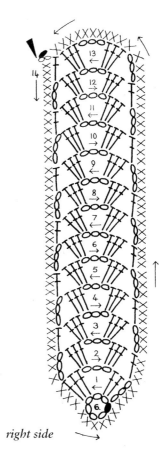

right side →

Examples of this bookmark with, both the plain and the contrasting edging, appear on page 54.

Before attaching the tassel(s), work the edge as follows: join the thread to a st beside the fastening-off point, work 1ch, 1dc in each dc, with 3dc together in the centre dc at the lower point of the bookmark. Use your imagination to ring the changes: the tassels can be replaced by an interesting bead or even a tiny bell.

These bookmarks, especially the straight ones, are perfect beginners' projects and yet they will make welcome gifts. The straight, as well as the cross-shaped bookmarks, can be worked with a contrasting edge.

LARGER BOOKMARK WITH A PICOT EDGE
(see photograph on page 57).

Approximate length, excluding ribbon: 5½ in / 14 cm

MATERIALS. Oddment of DMC Cébélia crochet cotton No 10 – dark red 816, a 1.75 mm crochet hook, 12 in / 30 cm of ribbon

Follow the instructions for the small bookmark, as given on page 53, but work a total of 17 rows. **Do not fasten off.**

Round 18 2ch, 3dc in first sp, *3dc in next sp. Repeat from* along the 1st long side, round the lower point of the bookmark, along the other long side and across the top edge, as shown on the diagram for the small bookmark. End with a sl st to the 2nd of 2ch at the start of edging.

Round 19 (picot edging) Use a **1.25 mm** crochet hook for this last round. This will ensure a neater finish. 5ch, a sl st to the 3rd ch from hook (1 x 3ch picot is now made), *1dc in each next 3dc, work 1 x 3ch picot, repeat from* till the end of the round. End with 1dc in last 3sts, sl st to base of 1st picot. Fasten off, sew in tail ends. Press lightly on the wrong side with a damp cloth. Slip-stitch to a length of ribbon. I used a cheerful tartan one, knotted one end and unravelled the threads to form a tassel.

CROSS-SHAPED BOOKMARK

Approximate length including tassel: 8 in / 20 cm

MATERIALS. Oddments of DMC Cébélia crochet cotton No 10 – white 5200, pale yellow 745 or pale blue 800, a 1.50 mm crochet hook

BEGIN. Following the diagram opposite, work 12ch, sl st to form a ring, 2ch, (12dc, 3ch, 4tr, 3ch, 4tr) in ring, 1tr in the 2nd of 2ch at beginning of the round, **turn.**

Row 2 3ch, miss 4tr, (4tr, 3ch, 4tr) in 3ch sp, miss 3tr, 1tr in next tr, 3ch, **turn.**

Row 3 to Row 7 Work as row 2, **turn.**

Row 8 Work 15ch, fairly tightly, miss (4tr, 3ch, 3tr), sl st in next tr, **turn.**

Row 9 3ch (3tr, 3ch, 8tr, 3ch, 8tr, 3ch, 4tr) in 15ch sp, **turn.**

LEFT SECTION OF THE CROSS

Row 10 3ch, miss 3tr, (4tr, 3ch, 4tr) in 3ch sp, miss 3tr, 1tr in next tr, **turn.**

Row 11 3ch, miss 4tr, (4tr, 3ch, 4tr) in 3ch sp, miss 3tr, 1tr in next tr. **Fasten off.**

RIGHT SECTION OF THE CROSS

Row 12 Rejoin to 3rd of 3ch at the beginning of row 9, work 3ch, miss 3tr, (4tr, 3ch, 4tr) in 3ch sp, miss 3tr, 1tr in next tr, **turn.**

Row 13 3ch, miss 4tr, (4tr, 3ch, 4tr) in 3ch sp, miss 3tr, 1tr in next tr. **Fasten off.**

TOP SECTION OF THE CROSS

Row 14 Rejoin at the 5th of the 8tr on row 9, work 3ch, miss 3tr, (4tr, 3ch, 4tr) in 3ch sp, miss 3tr, 1tr in next tr, **turn.**

Row 15 3ch, miss 4tr, (4tr, 3ch, 4tr) in 3ch sp, miss 3tr, 1tr in next tr, **turn.**

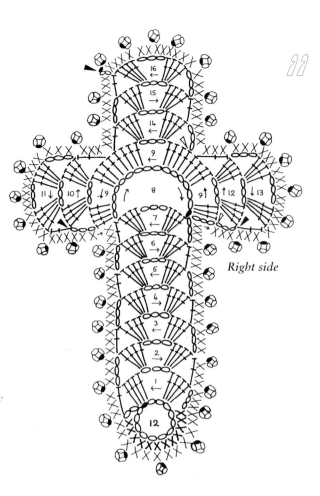

Diagram of the cross-shaped bookmark. As in the case of the other bookmarks, the edging of the little cross can be worked in a contrasting colour.

Row 16 As row 15, but **do not turn** at the end of the row. Unless you want to work a contrasting edge, **do not fasten off** at this point.

PICOT EDGING

If the edge is of the same colour as the cross, work down the left-hand side of the cross as follows: 2ch, (3dc, 1 x 3ch picot) in first sp, (3dc, 1 x 3ch picot) in next 3ch sp, 3dc, **no picot** in next sp, (3dc, 1 x 3ch picot) in first sp on **the left section** of the cross, (3dc, 1 x 3ch picot) in next 3ch sp, 1dc in each next 2tr, (1dc, 1 x 3ch picot) in next tr. Continue working this picot edging all around the cross, as shown on the diagram on page 55, checking the position of the picots carefully. End with a sl st to the 2ch at the start of edging. **Fasten off** and sew in all tail ends.

CONTRASTING COLOURED PICOT EDGE
Fasten off at the end of row 16, join the new colour to the last tr on row 16 (tie under top 2 threads). Begin with 2ch and work the picot edge as before, following the diagram carefully. End with a sl st to the 2ch at the start of edging. **Fasten off**, sew in all tail ends.

TO COMPLETE
Chains and tassels can also be added if you wish. For the tassels, refer to page 26. Press the finished bookmark lightly, using a damp cloth, pull gently into shape and pin on a board covered with cling film. Leave to dry.

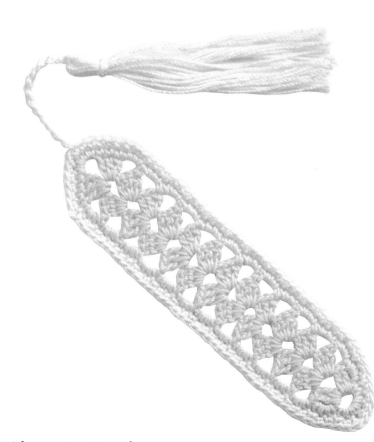

Straight bookmark with a contrasting edge

PRETTY POCHETTE

Approximate depth of crochet panel: 6½ in / 16.5 cm. When mounted up the pochette is 7 in / 18 cm deep and is large enough to contain an average-sized compact and a lipstick, keeping your handbag tidy.

MATERIALS. 25g DMC Cébélia crochet cotton No 10 – écru naturel, a 1.50 mm crochet hook, a Velcro dot and 1 small button

TENSION / GAUGE
The diameter of round 1 should be ½ in / 1.5 cm

WORKING NOTES
- Refer to the diagram opposite throughout and keep the tension firm and even.
- The motif is worked in the same direction on every round.
- Pay particular attention to the beginning and the end of each round, marking the sts where necessary.
- On the diagram, the **first** dc of each round is marked with a small dot up to round 13.
- You may find it helpful to colour each round on a photocopy of the diagram, alternating 2 colours to distinguish each round.

BEGIN. 6ch, sl st to form a ring.

Round 1 3ch (to count as a tr), 11tr in ring (12sts incl 3ch), sl st to the 3rd of 3ch to complete round. **Do not turn.**

Round 2 5ch, *miss 1tr, 1dc in next tr, 5ch, repeat from* 4 more times, sl st at the base of the 5ch at the begining of the round (6 x 5ch loops). **Note:** It helps to mark the first block of 3dc on the following round with a safety pin as a reminder of the beginning of each round.

Round 3 3dc in the first 5ch loop, 5ch, *3dc in next 5ch loop, 5ch, repeat from* 3 more times. **End** with 3dc in the last loop on this round, work 1dc in each of next 2dc, making a 5dc blk. (The completed 5dc blk marks the beginning of round 4.)

Round 4 5ch, *miss 1dc, 3dc in next loop, 1dc in each of the next 2dc, 5ch, repeat from* 3 more times. End with 3dc in the next loop, 1dc in each of the next 4dc, making a 7dc blk. (The completed 7dc blk marks the beginning of round 5.)

Round 5 5ch, *miss 1dc, 3dc in next loop, 1dc in each of the next 4dc, 5ch, repeat from* 3 more times. **End** with 3dc in next loop, 1dc in each of the next 6dc, making a 9dc blk.

Continue to increase blks by 2dc on next 3 rounds. Check the diagram at each round.

Round 6 Work 5 x 9dc blks.

Round 7 Work 5 x 11dc blks.

Round 8 Work 5 x 13dc blks. This round ends with the 5th of the 13 dc blks.

It is here that the blks of dc begin to decrease and there are now 4ch loops between the blks.

Round 9 *4ch, 1dc in next loop, 4ch, miss 1dc, 1dc in each of the next 11dc, leave the last dc unworked, repeat from* 4 more times (5 x 11dc blks).

Round 10 *4ch, 1dc in next loop, 4ch, 1dc in next loop, 4ch, miss 1dc, 1dc in each next 9dc, repeat from* 4 more times.

Round 11 *(4ch, 1dc in next loop) 3 times, 4ch, miss 1dc, 1dc in each next 7dc, repeat from* 4 more times.

Round 12 *(4ch, 1dc in next loop) 4 times, 4ch, miss 1dc, 1dc in each next 5dc, repeat from* 4 more times.

Round 13 *(4ch, 1dc in next loop) 5 times, 4ch, miss 1dc, 1dc in each next 3dc, repeat

from* 4 more times. The spiral design is complete.

Round 14 4ch (mark 4th ch with a safety pin, this ensures the correct placing of the sl st at the end of the round), 1dc in next loop, *(4ch, 1dc in next loop) 5 more times, 4ch, miss 1dc, 1htr in next dc, 4ch, miss 1dc, 1dc in next loop, repeat from* 3 more times. End with 4ch, 1dc in the next loop 5 times, 4ch, miss 1dc, 1htr in next dc, 4ch, sl st to the 4th of the 4ch (marked) at the beginning of the round.

Round 15 **Work firmly.** 1ch, 4dc in each of the next 2 loops, 5dc in next (corner) loop. Mark the centre dc of the completed 5dc group. *4dc in the next 6 loops, 5dc in the next (corner) loop, mark

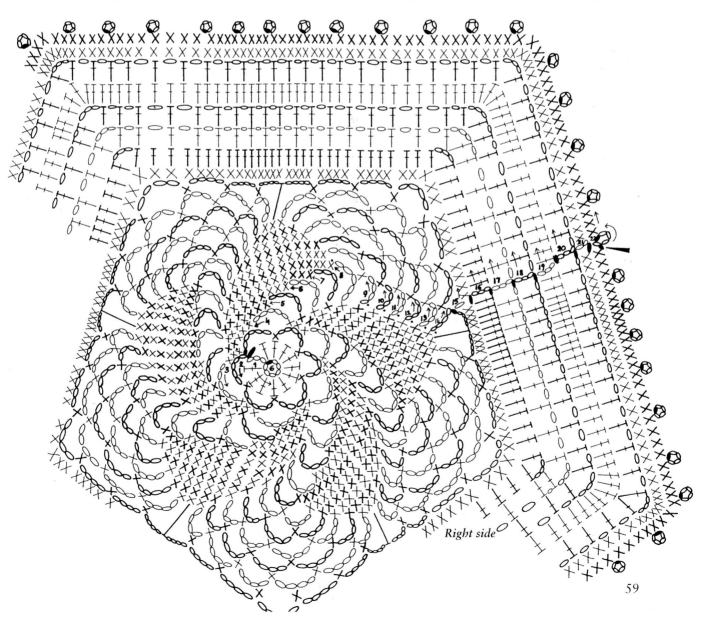

Right side

59

the centre dc as before, repeat from* 3 times. End with 4dc in the last 4 loops, sl st in the first dc at the beginning of this round.

Round 16 Work firmly. 3ch (to count as 1 tr), 1tr in each of the next 9dc, *work a corner group (1tr, 3ch, 1tr) in the next corner dc (marked), 1tr in each of the next 28dc, repeat from* 3 more times. End with (1tr, 3ch, 1tr) in the next corner dc, 1tr in remaining 18sts, sl st to the 3rd of the 3ch.

Round 17 4ch (to count as 1tr and 1ch), miss st at the base of 4ch and next tr, 1tr in next tr, *1ch, miss a tr, 1tr in next tr, repeat from* till 5sps made. Work 1ch, (1tr, 3ch, 1tr) in the next corner loop. *1ch, miss a tr, 1tr in next tr, repeat from* till 15 x 1ch sps from corner loop, 1ch, (1tr, 3ch, 1tr) in corner loop. Continue round the remaining sides. End with 1ch, miss a tr, sl st to the 3rd of 4ch at the beginning of the round. **All 5 sides should have 16 x 1ch sps between the corner loops.**

Round 18 4ch (to count as 1tr and 1ch), miss 1ch, 1tr in next tr, *1ch, miss 1ch, 1tr in next tr, repeat from* till 6sps made, 1ch, (1tr, 3ch, 1tr) in corner loop, *1ch, 1tr in next tr, repeat from* till 17 x 1ch sps from corner loop, 1ch, (1tr, 3ch, 1tr) in corner loop. Continue round the remaining sides. End with 1ch, a sl st to the 3rd of the 4ch at the beginning of the round. **All 5 sides should have 18 x 1ch sps between the corner loops.**

Round 19 3ch (to count as 1tr), *1tr in 1ch sp, 1tr in tr, repeat from* on all 5 sides, working 5tr in the corner loops (see diagram). Mark centre dc as before. End with 1tr in the last ch sp, sl st in the first tr (**not** the 3ch).

Round 20 4ch (to count as 1tr and 1ch), miss st at the base of the 4ch and the next tr, 1tr in next tr, *1ch, miss 1 st, 1tr in next tr, repeat from* till 8sps made, 3ch, 1tr in same st as last tr (1st corner loop). *1ch, miss a tr, 1tr in next tr, repeat from*, 3ch, 1tr in the same st as last tr (2nd corner). Continue till the end of the round, following the diagram. End with 1ch, sl st to the 3rd of the 4ch. **All 5 sides should have 21 x 1ch sps between the corner loops. Adjust if necessary.**

Round 21 Work firmly. 2ch (to count as 1dc) *1dc in sp, 1dc in tr, repeat from* on all 5 sides, working 5dc in corner loops. End with a sl st in the 2nd of the 2ch.

For a neater finish, work this last round using a 1.25 mm crochet hook.

Round 22 4ch, sl st to the first of 4ch (1 x 4ch picot is a completed picot), *1dc in each next 4dc, 1 x 4ch picot, repeat from* till the end of the round. End with a sl st to the base of the 1st picot.

You may have to 'cheat' a little and adjust the placing of the picots, so that they fall neatly at the corners of the work. Press lightly on the wrong side, using a damp cloth. Leave to dry.

Make up the pochette, using the pattern on page 17. Slip-stitch the crochet motif, or, as on the photographed example, use narrow embroidery ribbon and a tapestry needle to attach the lace to the bag (remember that you may need to remove it for washing). Tie the ends of the ribbon with a tiny bow. Attach a small Velcro dot to close the bag and add a pretty button.

BUTTERFLY & DAISY PANEL

Approximate size: 22 x 19 in / 56 x 49.5 cm

MATERIALS. 150 g DMC Cébélia crochet cotton No 10 – white 5200, a 1.50 mm crochet hook, fabric to back the panel or to make up the cushion cover

STITCHES, ABBREVIATIONS & SYMBOLS

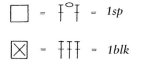

TENSION / GAUGE

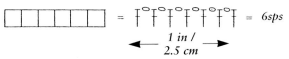

WORKING NOTES

- 1ch between trs on open mesh.
- Mark every 50th ch st with a safety pin. This avoids having to recount from the start, if you lose count on this long chain.
- It may help to colour each row as you work on a photocopy of the diagram.

BEGIN. 222ch (firmly). See diagram on pages 64-65.

Row 1   1tr in 6th ch from hook, *1ch, miss 1ch, 1tr in the next ch, continue from* to the end of the chain (109sps), 4ch, turn.
If the first row of the work appears loose or wavy, use a smaller hook to work the ch and the first row.
Row 2   Miss 1ch, 1tr in next tr, *1ch, miss 1ch, 1tr in the next ch, continue from* 4ch, turn.

Row 3   As row 2.

Row 4   Miss 1ch, 1tr in next tr, *1ch, miss 1ch, 1tr in next tr, repeat from* once more (until 3sps from start of row). 1tr in 1ch sp, 1tr in tr, repeat from* till 3sps remain at the end of the previous row. 1ch, miss 1ch, 1tr in next tr, 1ch, miss 1ch, 1tr in tr, 1ch, miss 1ch. End with 1tr in the 3rd of the 4ch (3sps at the end of the row), 4ch, turn.

From row 5   Continue to work blks and sps as shown on the graph diagram until all 109 rows are complete. **Do not fasten off.**

PANEL EDGING

With the right side of the work facing you, work 1dc in the first sp, *1dc in st, 1dc in sp, 1dc in st, 1 x 5ch picot. Repeat from*, working an extra 2dc in corners, till all 4 edges are complete. Fasten off, sew in tail ends.

TO COMPLETE

Press the panel lightly on the wrong side, using a damp cloth. Ease into shape and, if necessary, pin out on a large board, covered with cling film. Leave to dry. Make a backing for the filet panel, using a fabric of your choice. Put a channel at the back to enable you to slip in a hanging pole. The panel can also be mounted on a fabric-covered board. In both cases, use tiny slip stitches to attach the work to the backing. The panel can also be mounted up on a pillowcase – see our example on page 66.

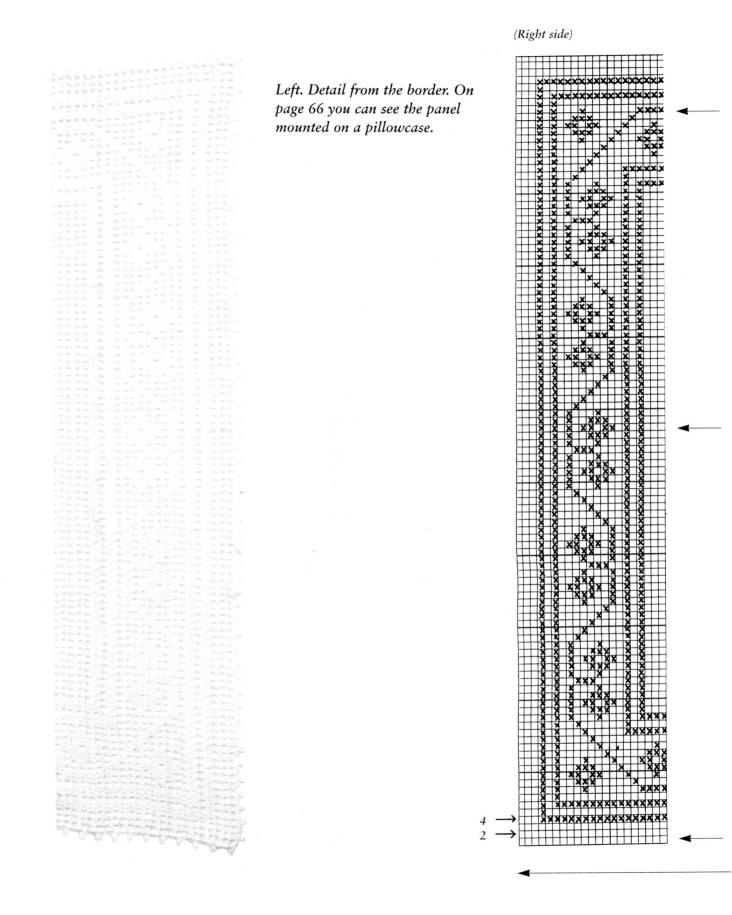

(Right side)

Left. Detail from the border. On page 66 you can see the panel mounted on a pillowcase.

4 →
2 →

Continuation of diagram on page 64

222ch (109 spaces)

← 5
← 3
← 1

KEY FOB OR SCISSOR KEEPER

Approximate size: 1 ½ in / 4 cm square

MATERIALS. Oddment of DMC Cébélia cotton No 10 – dark red 816, aqua 992, écru naturel, a 1.50 mm crochet hook, scraps of fine fabric, wadding or soft card

WORKING NOTES

- ◆ Work all chs and sts firmly, tightening each st as you work.

FRONT OF THE FOB (including rose motif, see diagram 1)

BEGIN. 6ch, sl st to form a ring.

Round 1   5ch, *1tr in ring, 2ch, repeat from* 6 more times. End with a sl st to the 3rd of 3ch (8 x 2ch sps made). Do **not** turn on this, or any of the following rounds.

Round 2   (1dc, 1htr, 1tr, 1htr, 1dc) in each 2ch sp till 8 petals are made. End with a sl st to the first dc.

Round 3   Continue to work in the same direction and, in the back of the first petal, work *4ch, 1dc around and under the stem of the next tr on round 1 (see diagram 2). Repeat from* till the end of the round. End with a sl st to the first ch at the beginning of the round (8 loops made).

DIAGRAM 1   *Front of the fob*

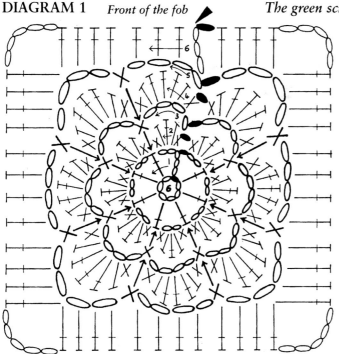

The green scissor keeper is shown from the back.

DIAGRAM 2

Stem or post (the vertical part of the stitch)

Round 4 (1dc, 1htr, 3tr, 1htr, 1dc) in each 4ch loop, till 8 petals are made. End with a sl st to the first dc.

Round 5 Working behind the petals: *4ch, carefully work 1dc around the stem of the dc on round 3. Repeat from* till the end of the round. End with a sl st to the first of 4ch (8 loops made).

Round 6 (3ch, 3tr) in the first loop, *(4tr, 5ch, 4tr) in next loop, 4tr in the next loop, repeat from* 2 more times. End with (4tr, 5ch, 4tr) in the last loop, sl st to 3rd of 3ch. Fasten off, sew in tail ends.

BACK OF THE FOB (see diagram 3)

BEGIN. 6ch, sl st to form a ring.

Round 1 3ch (to count as 1tr), 15tr in ring (16 sts including 3ch), sl st to the 3rd of 3ch, 3ch, turn.

Round 2 1tr in each of the next 3tr, *5ch, 1tr in each of the next 4tr, repeat from* 2 more times. End with 5ch, sl st to the 3rd of 3ch, 3ch, turn.

DIAGRAM 3   *Back of the fob or scissor keeper*

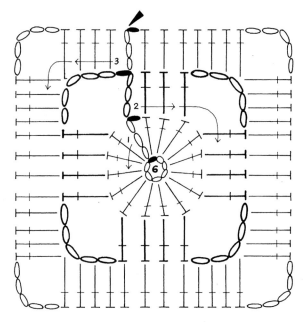

Round 3 (4tr, 5ch, 4tr) in the corner loop, *1tr in each of the next 4tr, (4tr, 5ch, 4tr) in the next corner loop, repeat from* 2 more times. End with 1tr in each of the remaining 3tr, sl st to the 3rd of 3ch. Fasten off, sew in tail ends.

INNER PAD
Cut a square of thin wadding slightly smaller than the crochet pouch. Cover in a fine material of your choice. The wadding can be replaced by a square of card for a firmer and flatter finish to the fob.

TO COMPLETE
Press the front and the back of the work lightly, opening out the petals of the Irish rose and easing into 2 neat square shapes of equal size. With wrong sides together, and with the rose motif facing you, tie the thread once through the back and the front of any 2 corner loops, linking the 2 sections. Use a smaller hook to give a neat, firm edge to your work. Join the sections together by inserting the hook in the same corner loops and pulling the thread through to make a working loop.

Work 2ch, 2dc in the same corner loops. Insert the hook carefully under the top 2 threads of the first tr on the rose motif and through the top 2 threads of the opposite tr on the back section, complete 1dc st. Continue to link the next 11tr along this first edge in the same way till you reach the next corner space, *5dc in the corner loop, link the next 12tr as before, repeat from* once more. Hold the loop with a safety pin. Insert the pad into the casing, remove the safety pin. Link the 2 edges of the remaining side together, as before. End with 2dc in the last corner loop, sl st to the 2nd of 2ch.

Do **not** fasten off. Work 100ch, firmly, a sl st in the st at the base of the 100ch, cut the thread, pass the tail end back through the working loop, pull tight to secure. Sew in tail ends.

PRETTY FANS FOR A GUEST TOWEL

Approximate size: each border measures 16 in / 41 cm (2 per towel). The length can be adjusted to fit the towel

MATERIALS. 25 g DMC Cébélia crochet cotton No 10 – écru teint 712, a 1.50 mm crochet hook, a guest towel – approximately 25 x 16 in / 63 x 41cm

SPECIAL STITCHES

 = *5 loop puff stitch (instructions on page 13)*

TENSION / GAUGE

One full 'fan' motif measures 2¼ in / 6 cm along the straight edge and one 'half fan' 1¼ in / 3 cm. Make a sample which includes both the full and the half fans. Measure it carefully to calculate the length of the border (see working notes below). Compare it with the width of the towel. If necessary, reduce or increase the size of the hook until you arrive at the correct length for the towel.

WORKING NOTES

◆ The border begins with one full fan and continues with half fans, hence multiples of half fans are required. The edging is added once the length of fan motifs is complete.

◆ Work **all** chs and sts firmly and follow the diagram throughout the work.

BEGIN. 9ch, sl st to form a ring.

Row 1 2ch, 11htr in ring, 4ch, turn.

Note: This round should fill only half the ring, leaving the remaining ch to form the straight edge of the fan border.

Row 2 Miss st at the base of 4ch and next st, 1tr in the next st, *1ch, 1tr in the next st, repeat from*. End with last tr in the 2tch on the row before (10 x 1ch sps made), 5ch, turn.

Row 3 *1 x 5 loop puff st in 1ch sp, 2ch, repeat from* till 10 puff sts made. End with 2ch, 1tr in the 3rd of 4ch on the row before, 6ch, turn.

Row 4 1tr in st on top of puff st (under 2 threads), *3ch, miss 2ch, 1tr in st on top of next puff st, repeat from*. End with 3ch, 1tr in 3rd of 5ch (11 x 3ch sps made), turn.

Round 5 Work *(1dc, 1htr, 1tr, 1htr, 1dc) in 3ch sp, one shell made. Repeat from* in each 3ch sp (11 shells). This completes one whole

DIAGRAM 1   *Right side*

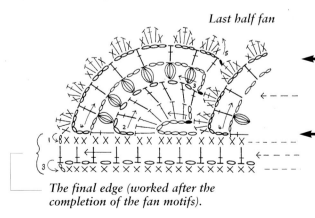

Last half fan

The final edge (worked after the completion of the fan motifs).

70

fan. Continue, adding half-fan motifs to complete the required length, as follows:

FIRST HALF FAN
Work 9ch, turn, sl st to the centre tr of the first shell, 2ch, turn.

Row 1 7htr in the 9ch loop, 4ch, turn.

Row Miss st at the base of the 4ch and next st, *1tr in next st, 1ch, repeat from* until 6 x 1ch sps, omit last ch st, sl st to the centre tr of the next shell, 5ch, turn.

Row 3 1 x 5 loop puff st in the first 1ch sp, *2ch, miss 1tr, 1 x 5 loop puff st in the next 1ch sp, repeat from* till 6 puff sts are made. End with 2ch, 1tr in the 3rd of 4ch, 6ch, turn.

Row 4 1tr in st on top of puff st, *3ch, miss 2ch, 1tr in st on top of next puff st, repeat from*. End with 3ch, 1tr in 3rd of 5ch (7 x 3ch sps made), sl st to centre tr of the next shell, turn.

Row 5 (1dc, 1htr, 1tr, 1htr, 1dc) in each 3ch sp (7 shells made). **Note:** This completes 1 half fan. Check your tension once again and make sure it is the same as in the sample you worked at the beginning. Once the required number of repeats is complete, hold the working loop with a safety pin. Press lightly with a steam iron, easing the lace to the required length. Leave to dry.

FINAL EDGE
Turn border upside down in readiness to work along the straight edge.

Row 1 2ch, *1dc in dc, 2dc in each next 3sps, 2dc in the side of htr, 4dc in next ch sp (13dc over the length of half fan, see diagram). Repeat from* over each **half fan**. Over last **full** fan, work 1dc in dc, 2dc in each of the next 3sps, 2dc in the side of htr, 4dc in next sp, 2dc in the side of 2ch, 2dc in each of the next 3sps, 1dc in dc, 4ch, turn.

Row 2 Miss st at base of 4ch *1tr in next st, 1ch, miss a st, repeat from* to the end. End with 1tr in last st. Adjust placing of last tr if necessary to complete the row, 2ch, turn.

Row 3 *1dc in 1ch sp, 1dc in tr, repeat from* to the end. End with 1dc in last sp and 1dc in the 3rd of 4tch. Fasten off, sew in tail ends. Make an identical border for the other end of the towel.

TO COMPLETE
Press the two lengths of lace lightly, using a steam iron. Pin out on a board covered with cling film, easing the lace to the length required, and leave to dry. Pin the borders carefully along each end of the guest towel: the lace should overlap slightly over the edge of towel. Ease to fit. Slip-stitch into place.

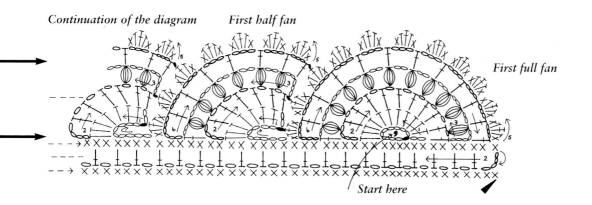

Continuation of the diagram   *First half fan*

First full fan

Start here

This guest towel will make someone a lovely present or give a touch of bygone elegance to a romantic bathroom.

BREAD BASKET LINER

Approximate size of open liner: 16 in / 40.5 cm square

MATERIALS. 100 g DMC Cébélia crochet cotton No 10 – green 699, a 1.50 mm crochet hook, a bread basket about 12 in / 31 cm square

STITCHES, ABBREVIATIONS & SYMBOLS

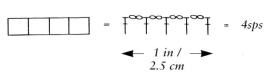

TENSION / GAUGE

WORKING NOTES

◆ 2ch between trs on open mesh.
◆ The square centre section of the liner is worked first, then the 4 triangular flaps.
◆ In the centre square section, all rounds start with 5ch, except for round 2. All rounds finish with 2ch and 1tr in centre ch of 5ch, except for round 2. All rounds are worked in the same direction within the centre square.
◆ Keep the tension firm and even and follow the stitch diagram as you work.

CENTRE SQUARE (see diagram on page 74)

BEGIN 6ch, sl st to form a ring.

Round 1 5ch (to count as 1tr and 2ch), 1tr in the ring, *5ch, 1tr in the ring, 2ch, 1tr in the ring, repeat from* 2 more times. End with 2ch, 1tr in the 3rd of 5ch (8sps forming a square). Do not turn.

Round 2 3ch, 2tr in sp, 1tr in the same ch as the last tr on round 1, 2tr in next sp, 1tr in tr, *(3tr, 5ch, 3tr) in 5ch sp, 1tr in tr, 2tr in the next sp, 1tr in tr, repeat from* 2 more times. End with 2tr in 2ch sp, 1tr in tr, 2ch, 1tr in the 3rd of 3ch. Do not turn.

Round 3 5ch, 1tr in the same ch as the last tr (the space just formed is the start of round 3). **Note:** Mark this first space with a safety pin. Remove and replace this marker as you start each of the next 19 rounds. The space count will not match the other 3 sides till the last space on the round is made. *2ch, miss 2tr, 1tr in each next 4tr, 2ch, miss 2tr, 1tr in next tr, 2ch, miss 2ch, (1tr, 5ch, 1tr) in the centre ch of 5ch, 2ch, miss 2ch, 1tr in tr, repeat from* 2 more times, 2ch, miss 2tr, 1tr in each of the next 4tr, 2ch, miss 2tr, 1tr in next tr, 2ch, miss 2ch, 1tr in next tr. End with 2ch, miss 2ch, 1tr in the centre ch of 5ch (hook under 2 threads if possible).

Note: The side facing you is the right side of the work, mark the **wrong** side with a contrast thread for future reference.

Round 4 5ch, 1tr in same ch as last tr (remove and replace the safety pin in the new 5ch sp as before). *2ch, miss 2ch, 1tr in next tr. Continue working a round of open meshes. End with 2ch, 1tr in the centre ch of 5ch, at the beginning of the round.

Round 5   As round 4.

Round 6   Start of the ivy leaf design. Work all tr blks and chs firmly and evenly to keep the work flat. Several blocks together are difficult to define, especially blocks over blocks, try multiplying the number of blocks on the graph by 3 and adding 1. Remember to count the first tr. Continue with round 6 as follows: 5ch, 1tr in same st as last tr (mark this new space as before), 2ch, miss 2ch, 1tr in next tr, *2tr in sp, 1tr in next tr, repeat from* 4 more times (5blks made). This is the start of the first ivy leaf.

Continue around the remaining 3 sides, as shown in diagram 1, ensuring that the first row

of each ivy leaf is correctly positioned. End with 2ch, 1tr in the centre ch of 5ch.

Round 7 to round 22   See diagram 2.
Note: Every few rounds, make sure that the work lies flat. If satisfactory, press lightly with a steam iron and ease into shape. Allow to dry on a flat surface, then continue. If the work is not flat, continuing will only the problem worse. Unpick and start again, tightening up all chs and sts as you work: maintaining a firm and even tension throughout the work is essential. The last row of the centre square should have 45 sps. **Do not fasten off.** Hold the loop with a safety pin.

FOLD-OVER FLAPS (Diagram 3 shows in detail the beginning and the end of the rows.)

WORKING NOTES
◆   The flaps are added to the centre square

DIAGRAM **1** *(Right side) Stitch detail of the centre square, showing the start and finish of each round.*

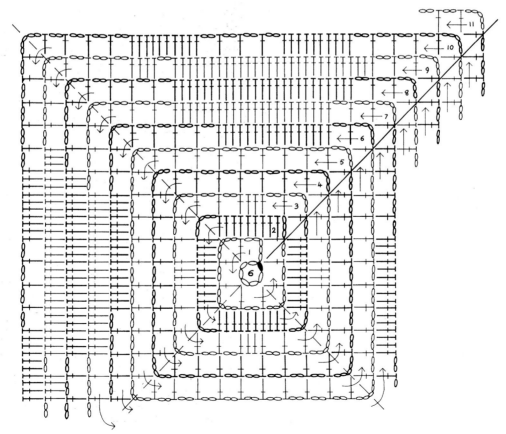

individually, so follow the diagram with extra care as you change direction on each row.

◆ The ivy leaf design is reversed on the flap.

◆ Work straight for the first 8 rows, then begin to decrease at the beginning and the end of each row, finishing with 1 block at the point of the flap.

◆ Work all turning chains quite firmly.

◆ It may be helpful to colour each row on a photocopy of the diagram as you work.

FIRST FLAP

With right side facing, remove the safety pin

DIAGRAM **2**
(Right side)

Continue from here with first fold-over flap.

Rejoin here for second fold-over flap.

Rejoin here for fourth fold-over flap.

Rejoin here for third fold-over flap.

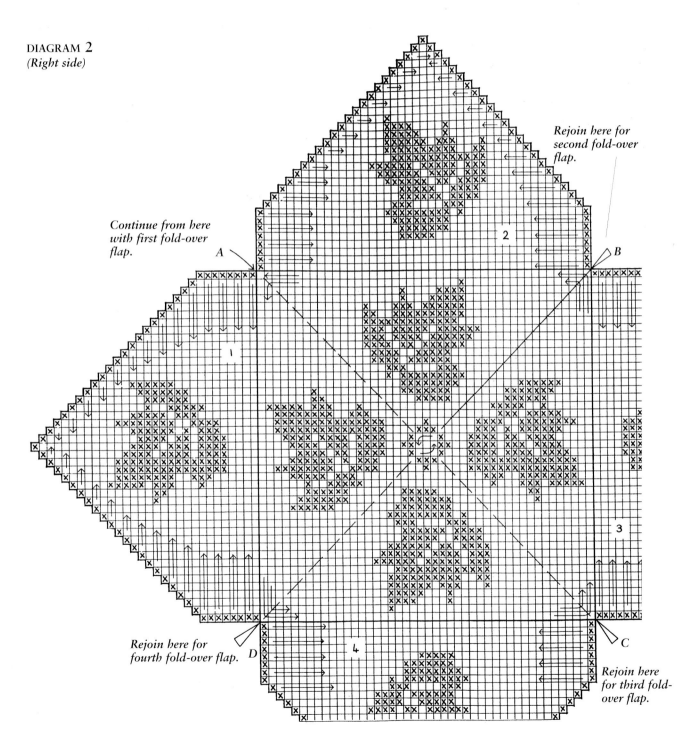

and insert the hook in the working loop. Continue from point **A** on diagram 2. For stitch detail, see also diagram 3.

Row 1 3ch (to count as 1tr), 2tr in 2ch sp, 1tr in next tr, *2ch, miss 2ch, 1tr in next tr, repeat from* to the last space but one. End with 3tr in the last sp, 3ch, turn.

Row 2 1tr in each 3tr, *2ch, miss 2ch, 1tr in next tr, repeat from* to the end of the row. End with 1tr in each of the last 3tr and 1tr in 3tch, 3ch, turn.

Row 3 and row 4 As row 2, turn.

Row 5 Start of the ivy leaf design. Work tr blks extra firmly. 1tr in each of next 3tr, *2ch, miss 2ch, 1tr in next tr, repeat from* till 20 sps are made, *2tr in 2ch sp, 1tr in next tr, repeat from* till 5 blks are made. *2ch, miss 2ch, 1tr in next tr, repeat from* till 18 sps are made. End with 1tr in each of the last 3tr and 1tr in 3tch, 3ch, turn.

Row 6, row 7 and row 8 As shown on diagram

3, omit 3ch at the end of the row 8, turn.

Row 9 First row of decreases, see diagram 3. Miss first tr, sl st in each of the next 3tr, 3ch, 2tr in 2ch sp, 1tr in next tr, *2ch, miss 2ch, 1tr in next tr, repeat from*, working blks and sps as shown on diagram 3. End with 2tr in the last sp, 1tr in next tr, turn.

Row 10 to row 29 Still following diagram 2, decrease at the beginning and the end of each row, as on row 9, turn.

Row 30 Miss first tr, sl st in each of the next 3tr, 3ch, 2tr in 2ch sp, 1tr in tr. Fasten off. **Turn the work over** till the right side faces you. Continue with the second flap.

SECOND FLAP
Join the thread by tying it once in the corner space B, follow instructions for 'flap 2' on diagram 2, starting from row 1.

THIRD FLAP
Join the thread to the corner space C, follow instructions for 'flap 2', as from row 1.

DIAGRAM 3 *(Right side)* *Note that the ivy leaf design is reversed on the flaps (see also diagram 2). The diagram below shows the stitch detail of the beginning and the end of each row and the start of the decreases on the flaps.*

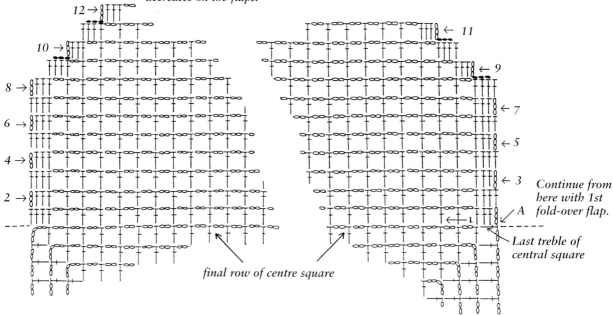

final row of centre square

Continue from here with 1st fold-over flap.

Last treble of central square

FOURTH FLAP

Join the thread to the corner space **D**, follow instructions for 'flap 2' as from row 1.

TO COMPLETE

Sew in all tail ends. Press lightly with a steam iron, using a damp cloth. Ease into shape, pin out on a large board covered in cling film. Leave to dry. Attach a chain and tassel to each end of the flaps. See page 26 for instructions.

This smaller version of the bread basket liner was produced using 100 g of DMC Cébélia crochet cotton No 20 and a 1.25 mm crochet hook. The finished work measures approximately 12½ in / 32 cm square.

ROSE NAPKIN RINGS

Approximate size: 2 in / 5 cm in diameter

MATERIALS. 50 g DMC Cébélia crochet cotton No 10 – écru naturel make 6 napkin rings, a 1.50 mm crochet hook

TENSION / GAUGE

Check: the length of the first row, excluding the picot edge, should be 2½ in / 6 cm.

WORKING NOTES

◆   Keep tension extra firm and even throughout.

BEGIN. 29ch firmly (see diagram 1).

Row 1   (1tr, 3ch, 1tr) in the 6th ch from hook, *miss 3ch (1tr, 3ch, 1tr) in the next ch st. Repeat from* 4 more times, miss 2ch, 1tr in the last ch st, 2ch, turn. See tension / gauge check above.

DIAGRAM **1** *(Right side)*

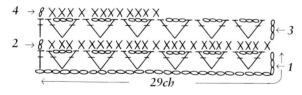

DIAGRAM **2** *(Wrong side) Detail of the last row and start of the finished edge with the picots in place*

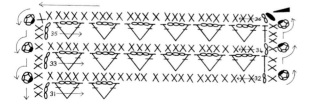

Row 2   3dc in 3ch sp, *1dc in sp between 2tr, 3dc in 3ch sp, repeat from* 4 more times. End with 1dc in the last sp, 3ch, turn.

Row 3   Miss st at the base of 3ch and next st, *(1tr, 3ch, 1tr) in next st, miss 3sts, repeat from* 5 more times. End with 1tr in the 2nd of 2ch, 2ch, turn. Rows 2 and 3 form the lace pattern.

Repeat rows 2 and 3 till 36 rows are complete, omitting the 3ch at the end of the last row. Do not fasten off. Mark the side of the work facing you with a contrast thread – this is the **wrong** side of the work.

PICOT EDGING (see diagram 2)
(The picot is worked on the 2 long sides only.). With the wrong side still facing you, turn the work and begin to work along the first long edge of the napkin ring. (1dc, 1 x 4ch picot, 2dc) in same sp as last dc, 1dc in the side of dc (row end), 1 x 4ch picot, *2dc in next sp, 1dc in the side of next dc, 1 x 4ch picot, repeat from* till you reach the next corner sp, 4dc in corner sp. If the edging is loose or wavy, try using a smaller hook.

Start along the first short side (no picots on short sides): *1dc between 2tr, 3dc in 3ch sp, repeat from* till the next corner, 4dc in the corner sp. Work along the other long side as follows: *1dc in the side of 2ch (row end), (1 x 4ch picot, 2dc) in next sp, repeat from* to the end of the long side. End with (3dc, 1 x 4ch picot) in the last sp,

sl st to 2ch at the beginning of the short side. Keep a long tail end for sewing the seam. Fasten off. Sew short tail end to the wrong side of the work.

Press the finished strip lightly on the wrong side before continuing. Do **not** sew the seam and make into a ring at this stage. The Irish rose motif must be worked first.

IRISH ROSE MOTIF (see diagram 3)

BEGIN. 6ch, sl st to form a ring.

Round 1   6ch (to count as 1tr and 3ch), 1tr in ring, *3ch, 1tr in ring, repeat from* till 5sps are made. End with 3ch, sl st to the 3rd of 3ch (6 spaces made). Do not turn.

Round 2   (1dc, 1htr, 3tr, 1htr, 1dc) in each 3ch loop till round, sl st to first dc (6 petals). Do not turn.

Round 3   Continue working in the same direction and, in the back, behind the first petal, work: *5ch, 1dc around and under the stem or post of the next tr on round 1 (see diagram 4), 5ch, repeat from* till round. End with a sl st to first ch at the beginning of the round (6 loops

made). Do not turn.

Round 4   (1dc, 1htr, 5tr, 1htr, 1dc) in each 5ch loop till round. End with a sl st to first dc. Do not turn.

Round 5   Working in the back, behind the 1st petal, *5ch, work a dc around and under dc on round 3 (make sure you position this st accurately), 5ch, repeat from* till round. End with a sl st to first of 5ch (6 loops made). Do not turn.

Round 6   (1dc, 1htr, 6tr, 1htr, 1dc) in each 5ch loop till round. End with a sl st to the first dc. Fasten off, sew in tail ends. The Irish rose motif is now complete.

MAKING UP THE NAPKIN RING

Pin the rose motif in the centre of the strip and on the right side of the work. Use matching sewing thread to attach the rose neatly into place. Stitch the side seam of the ring, working from the wrong side of the work and using the long tail end of thread. Turn the work so that the rose faces you and gently pull the petals into shape. Touch up with a steam iron, if necessary.

DIAGRAM 3 *(Right side)*

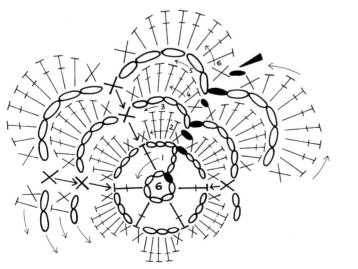

DIAGRAM 4
The stem or post (the vertical part of the stitch)

WALL HANGING

Approximate size of crochet panel: 30 x 5 in / 76 x 13 cm

MATERIALS. 75 g DMC Cébélia crochet cotton No 10 – dark red 816, a 1.50 mm crochet hook, suitable fabric for mounting the hanging

STITCHES, ABBREVIATIONS & SYMBOLS

TENSION / GAUGE

WORKING NOTES

◆ 1ch between trs on open mesh
◆ Refer to the diagram opposite as you work and keep the tension firm and even.

BEGIN. 56ch (see diagram 1).

Row 1 1tr in 6th ch from hook, *1ch, miss 1ch, 1tr in next ch, repeat from* to the end of the row (26sps), 4ch, turn.

Row 2 Miss 1ch, 1tr in next tr, *1ch, miss 1ch, 1tr in next tr, repeat from*. At the end, miss 1ch, 1tr in next ch, 4ch, turn.

Row 3 to row 7 As row 2.

Row 8 Miss 1ch, 1tr in next tr, *1ch, miss 1ch, 1tr in next tr, repeat from* till 7sps, 1tr in next sp, 1tr in next tr (one blk made), *1ch, miss

1ch, 1tr in next tr, repeat from* to the end of the row (18sps), 4ch, turn. Continue, following diagram 1 and working blks and sps till the grapevine motif is complete. Work 7 more rows of basic filet crochet mesh as explained in row 2, omitting the last 4ch on the final row (153 rows). Do not cut the thread. Hold the loop with a safety pin. Before continuing, press the work lightly on the wrong side, using a damp cloth.

EDGING

Remove the safety pin. With right side facing, work along the first **long side** of the crochet panel (see diagram 2 for stitch detail). Tighten each dc as you work the st.

BEGIN. 2ch, 2dc in corner sp, 2dc in each sp along the left-hand side of the panel, 5dc in the corner sp. Work along the lower edge of the panel as follows: 1dc in next tr, 1dc in sp, repeat from* to the next corner sp, 5dc in the corner sp, 2dc in each sp along the right hand side of the panel, 5dc in the corner sp. Work along the top edge as follows: *1dc in next tr, 1dc in sp, repeat from* to the last corner sp, sl st to the 2nd of 2ch at the start of edging, turn.

Change to a hook one size smaller for the final round. Work firmly as follows: *3ch, miss a st, 1dc in next st, repeat from* on all 4 sides. This last round should lie flat. End with a sl st to the base of the 3ch at the beginning of the round. Fasten off, sew in tail ends to the wrong side of the panel.

The panel can be mounted on a piece of fabric, as illustrated on page 84, or framed (avoid glass).

DIAGRAM 1
(Right side)

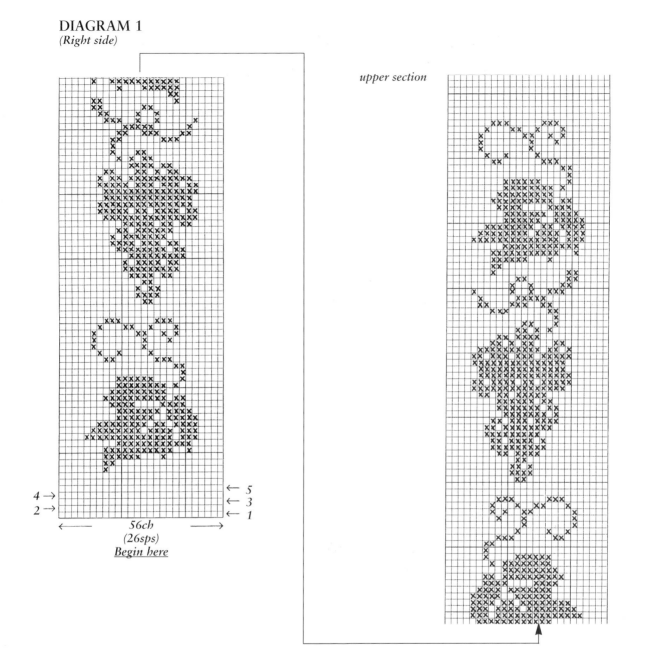

upper section

4 →   ← 5
2 →   ← 3
     ← 1

56ch
(26sps)
Begin here

DIAGRAM **2** *(Right side) Stitch detail of the start and finish of the edging*

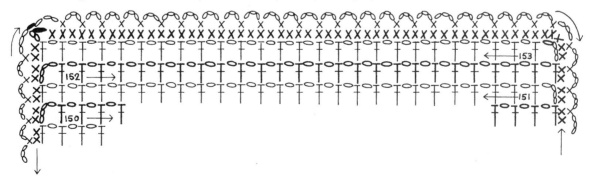

← 153
152 →
← 151
150 →

TISSUE BOX COVER

Approximate size: 9 x 4⅜ x 2¾ in / 23 x 11 x 7 cm. The size of the boxes may vary slightly according to the brand. By adjusting the tension, the pattern can be made to fit most rectangular boxes, containing 150 tissues.

MATERIALS. 75 g DMC Cébélia crochet cotton No10 – white 5200 (the quantity given allows for slight variations in box sizes), a 1.50 mm crochet hook, 1 standard box of 150 tissues

STITCHES, ABBREVIATIONS & SYMBOLS

TENSION / GAUGE

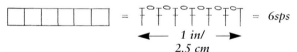

WORKING NOTES

◆ 1ch between trs on open mesh

◆ It is advisable to make a sample to check the tension: 26ch, work a basic mesh over 5 or 6 rows. If necessary, change the hook size to achieve the correct number of spaces over a given measurement. (The tension given applies to the box measurements above.)

◆ Follow the diagrams carefully and keep the tension firm and even throughout.

◆ An odd number of spaces is required for the butterfly and the bow designs on the sides of the box.

◆ To improve the shape of the last space at the end of each row, try missing 2ch instead of 1ch, the last tr in the next ch st and working always under 2 threads.

STAGE ONE – TOP PANELS OF THE BOX

Follow diagram 1 – you will see that the top of the box is formed by 2 panels, bearing the butterfly design.

BEGIN

First panel: 106ch, worked fairly tight.

DIAGRAM 1 *(Right side) The panels which will form the top of the box.*

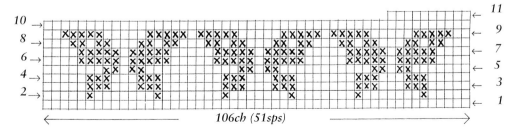

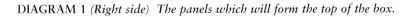

Row 1 1tr in the 6th ch from hook, *1ch, miss 1ch, 1tr in next ch, repeat from* to the end of the row (51sps), 4ch, turn. At this stage check that the tension is correct and that your first row measures **exactly** the same as the top of the box. If this first row is too long or loose, try using a smaller hook; if too short and tight, use a hook one size bigger. **It is vital** to ensure that this first row is the correct length and has the required number of spaces, or you may discover at the end of all your effort, that the finished cover does not fit!

Row 2 Miss 1ch, 1tr in the next tr, *1ch, miss 1ch, 1tr in the next ch, repeat from* till 5sps from beginning of row, 1tr in next sp, 1tr in tr (1blk made), the first block of the butterfly design. Continue along this row, following the butterfly design on diagram 1. At the end of the row, miss 1ch, 1tr in next ch, 4ch, turn.

Row 3 to row 9 will complete the butterfly design.

Row 10 Work 1 more row of filet crochet mesh, beyond the butterfly design. These 10 rows should be 2 in / 5 cm deep.

Row 11 Work a **short** row as follows: miss 1ch, 1tr in next tr, *1ch, miss 1ch, 1tr in the next ch, repeat from* till 10 sps from the beginning of the row. Leave a long tail end and fasten off.

SECOND PANEL
Work exactly as the first.

Press both butterfly panels lightly, using a damp cloth. Before sewing together, check that both panels, when placed together as in diagram 2, fit the top of the box **exactly**. Ensure that the short 10sp rows are placed towards the centre of the box. This will form the opening to pull out the handkerchiefs.

Using the cotton tail, stitch the short 10sp row on panel 1 to the opposite 10sps on panel 2, matching tr to tr and sp to sp. A neat seam can be achieved if you take the needle under the top 2 threads of the trs as you sew them together. Do **not** sew too tightly. Repeat with the other 10sp section. Sew in all tail ends. For future reference mark the wrong side of the completed panels with a contrast thread. Press lightly with a steam iron on the wrong side, using a damp cloth. Ease to fit the top of the box.

STAGE TWO – SIDE PANELS
(See diagram 4 on page 88 for the bow design.)

WORKING NOTES
◆ The 4 sides of the cover are worked in one continuous section and the bows are worked starting from the top of the design.
◆ On round 1 work to a firmer tension by tightening each dc as you complete the st, especially on the long sides
◆ Also on round 1, it is important to mark the centre dc of the 5dc, at each corner, with a safety pin

BEGIN. With right side facing (see diagram 3), tie

DIAGRAM **2** *Position of the 2 top panels, ready for assembly*

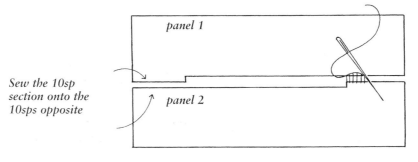

Sew the 10sp section onto the 10sps opposite

panel 1

panel 2

the thread into the top left-hand corner, as shown.

Round 1   Short side. Work firmly, 1ch, 5dc beside 1ch in the first corner sp, **mark the centre dc** under the top 2 threads, *2dc in each next 10sps, **work 1dc on sewn seam**, 2dc in the remaining 9sps, 5dc in corner sp, **mark centre dc** (43sts between marked corner sts on short side). **Long side.** 1dc in first sp, 2dc in each remaining sp till you reach the next corner sp, 5dc in the next corner sp, **mark centre dc** (101sts between the marked corner sts on the long side). Repeat from* on remaining 2 sides, remember: 1dc on sewn seam and **1dc only** in first sp on long side. Match st numbers between marked sts on opposite sides. Omit the 5dc in the last corner sp. End with a sl st to first dc of the corner group. Sl st **again** in each next 2 dc, remove the marker, 4ch, turn.

Round 2   Long side. Start of the filet crochet mesh. Wrong side facing, miss st at the base of 4ch and next st, 1tr in the next st, *1ch, miss 1dc, 1tr in the next dc, repeat from* till you reach the marked st at the next corner. Remove marker. Work 1ch, miss 1dc, (1tr, 1ch, 1tr) in the corner st, replace marker in the newly formed corner sp (51sps excluding the corner sp). **Short side.** *1ch, miss 1dc, 1tr in next st, repeat from* till you reach the marked st at the next corner. Remove the marker, work 1ch, miss 1dc (1tr, 1ch, 1tr) in the corner st, replace the marker in the newly formed corner sp (22sps, excluding the corner sps). Continue round the remaining 2 sides, marking the **new** corner sp. End with 1ch, miss 1dc, 1tr at the base of 4ch at the beginning of the round, 1ch, sl st to 3rd of 4ch. This last sp forms a corner sp mark this as before, 4ch, turn. Your work will now begin to turn down on all 4 sides.

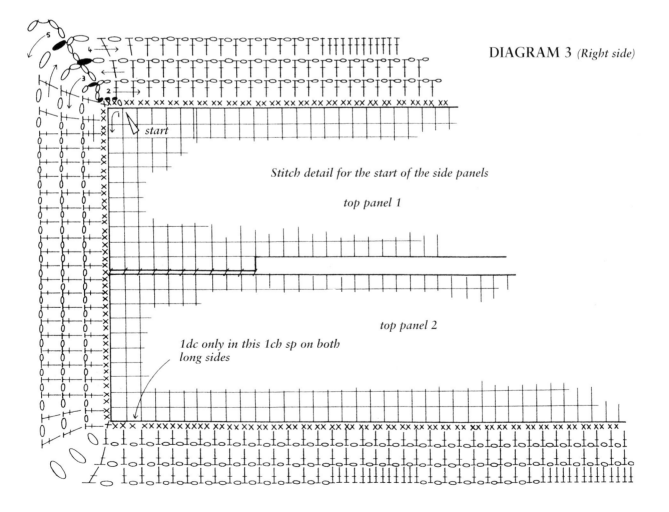

DIAGRAM 3 (*Right side*)

start

Stitch detail for the start of the side panels

top panel 1

top panel 2

1dc only in this 1ch sp on both long sides

Round 3   Short side. Right side facing, miss 1ch, 1tr in **next** tr, **mark** new corner sp, *1ch, miss 1ch, 1tr in the next tr, repeat from* till 22sps from the corner. Remove the marker, work 1ch, miss 1ch, 1tr in the next tr, **mark** the new corner sp, *1ch, miss 1ch, 1tr in next tr, repeat from* till 51 sps from the corner, remove the marker, 1ch, miss 1ch, 1tr in next tr, **mark** the new corner sp. Continue round the last 2 sides, marking the new corner sp as before. End with 1ch, sl st to the 3rd of 4ch, 4ch, turn.

Note: The next round is the start of the bow design, which appears on the long sides only and is worked from the top of the cover down. You may find it easier to follow if you photocopy diagram 4 and turn it upside down. The short sides of the cover are worked in basic mesh.

Round 4   Long side. Wrong side facing, miss 1ch, 1tr in next tr, *1ch, miss 1ch, 1tr in next tr, repeat from* till 15sps made, *1tr in the next sp, 1tr in tr, repeat from* till 6blks are made (start of bow design). Continue to work blks and sps according to diagram 4, working the 4 sides as one complete round. End each round with a sl st to the 3rd of 4ch, 4ch, turn. Continue to mark the corners as a useful guide, turning the work after each round.

Round 5 to round 12   complete the bow design. End each round with a sl st to the 3rd of 4ch, 4ch, turn.

Round 13   Miss 1ch, 1tr in next tr, *1ch, miss 1ch, 1tr in next tr, repeat from* till round all 4 sides. End with a sl st to the 3rd of 4ch, 4ch, turn. Hold the loop with a safety pin.

At this stage, try the cover on the box, ease to fit neatly at the corners. The cover should almost reach the bottom edge of the box, leaving approximately ¼ in / 6 mm, i.e. just enough space to add the final picot edge. Remove the safety pin and continue. **If the side panels are too short**, repeat round 13 once more or till the required depth is achieved. Then add the final picot edge, changing to a smaller hook. Work this last round with the **wrong** side of the work facing you to emphasize the picot.

PICOT EDGING
4ch, sl st to the first of 4ch, pull tight (1 x 4ch picot made), 1dc in 1ch sp, 1dc in next tr, 1dc in next 1ch sp, 1dc in next tr, repeat from till round all 4 sides. End with a sl st to the base of the first picot. Fasten off.

THE EDGE TO THE CENTRAL OPENING
With right side facing, tie the thread to a 1ch sp at the right-hand side of the opening. Work 1ch, 2dc in each sp all round the opening. Sl st to the first dc at the beginning of the round. Fasten off, sew in all tail ends.

TO COMPLETE
Press lightly, using a damp cloth, making sure you do not stretch the cover. Make a silk lining to go under the cover – see instructions on page 16.

DIAGRAM 4 *(Right side) long side panels*

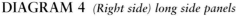

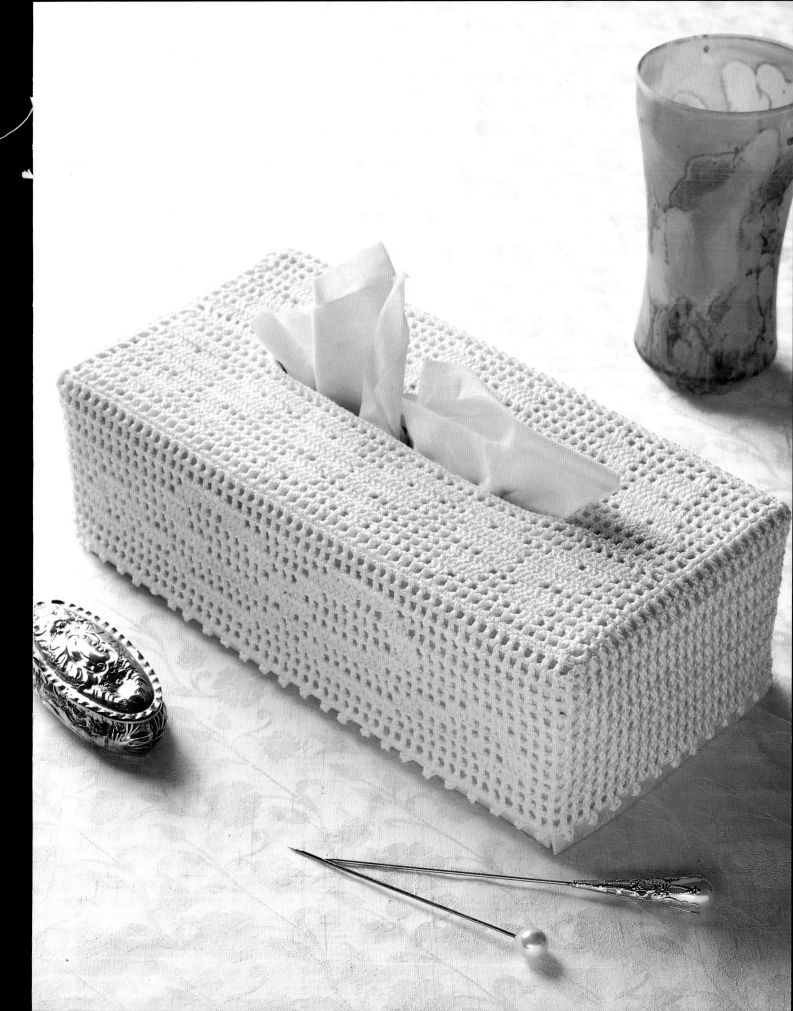

MAGNOLIA TABLE CLOTH

Approximate size of tablecloth: 39 in / 100 cm square (including chevron border). Each motif measures 6 in / 15 cm square and the border is 3 in / 8 cm deep.

MATERIALS. 450 g DMC Cébélia crochet cotton No 10 – white 5200 to make the table cloth shown on page 95, which is composed of 36 motifs, and its border (100g will yield at least 9 motifs), a 1.50 mm crochet hook, a box of small safety pins

SPECIAL STITCHES

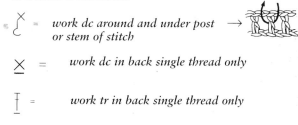

= *work dc around and under post or stem of stitch*

X = *work dc in back single thread only*

= *work tr in back single thread only*

= *single picot group*

= *double picot group*

= *open dtr 'shell'*

WORKING NOTES

◆ The final size of the work depends on the number of motifs. Multiply the size of a single motif, adding the width of the border, to decide how many you will need to produce the table cloth or bedspread of your choice.

◆ Always work under the top 2 threads of all sts unless otherwise stated.

◆ Work all stitches and chains firmly and follow the diagram opposite as you work.

◆ Use safety pins to mark stitches, as indicated in the text to ensure the accurate placing of stitches.

BEGIN. 10ch, sl st to form a ring.

Round 1 1ch, 12dc in ring, sl st to first dc. Do not turn.

The petals are worked individually – follow diagram 1 very carefully.

Round 2   First petal: 14ch, 1dc in the 3rd ch from hook, 1htr in next ch, 1tr in each next 2ch, 1dtr in each next 5ch, 1tr in each next 2ch, 1htr in last ch, sl st to first dc on round 1, 1ch, turn so that the wrong side of the work faces you, 1dc around/under the stem of each next 6sts, 8ch (start of the second petal).

Second petal: *1dc in 3rd ch from hook, 1htr in next ch, 1tr in each next 2ch, 1dtr in each next 2ch. Turn the work over till right side facing, continue along the remainder of the second petal: 1dtr in each next 3dc, 1tr in each next 2dc, 1htr in last dc, sl st to the next dc on round 1, 1ch, turn the work so that the wrong side faces you, 1dc around/under stem of each next 6sts, 8ch (start of the next petal).
Work the other 10 petals as from* of the **second** petal, but **omitting** 8ch after the 6dc on the final petal. Leave a long tail end and fasten off. Turn work to the wrong side and use the tail end to sew the 6dc on the **last** petal to the 6sts on the **first** petal, matching each stitch with the stitch opposite. Sew from the middle of the petals towards the centre of the flower. This should

leave a ridge on the right side to match the other petals. Sew the tail ends to the wrong side. Steam press very lightly on the wrong side to straighten out the petals.

Round 3 Right side facing. Insert the hook under 2 threads at the point of any of the petals, draw the cotton tail through and tie once. Insert the hook in the same place and draw through a working loop, 1ch, 1dc beside 1ch, *8ch (tight), 1dc in the next petal point, 8ch, 1dc in the next petal point, 1ch, **turn**, (4dc, 4ch, 4dc) in 8ch loop, 1dc in dc, 2ch, **turn**, **1dtr in 4ch loop, 2ch, repeat from** 6 more times, miss 4dc, sl st in the next st (8 x 2ch sps made = open dtr 'shell'), 8ch, 1dc in the next petal point, repeat from* till the end of the round. End with a sl st to the first dc at the beginning of the round.

Round 4 8ch (to count as 1tr and 5ch), *miss 8ch, 1dtr in st on the next petal point, see

diagram 1. 5ch, miss (2ch, 1dtr, 2ch), 1tr in the next dtr, 5ch, miss (2ch, 1dtr, 2ch). Work (1tr, 5ch, 1tr) in next dtr (corner group made), 5ch, miss (2ch, 1dtr, 2ch) 1tr in next dtr, 5ch, miss (2ch, 1dtr, 2ch), 1dtr in st on the next petal point, 5ch, miss 8ch, 1tr in st on next petal point, 5ch. Repeat from* 3 more times. Omit the final tr and 5ch on the last repeat. End with a sl st to the 3rd of 8ch at the beginning of the round.

Round 5 4ch, miss st at the base of 4ch, 1tr in next ch, 1ch, miss 1ch, 1tr in next ch, 1ch, miss 1ch, 1tr in dtr, *1ch, miss 1ch, 1tr in next ch, 1ch, miss 1ch, 1tr in next ch, 1ch, miss 1ch, 1tr in next tr, repeat from* once more. Work the corner group as follows: 1ch, miss 1ch, 1tr in next ch, 1ch, 1tr in the **next** ch, **mark** this corner with a safety pin (under 2 threads), 1ch, 1tr in the **next** ch, 1ch, **miss** 1ch, 1tr in next tr, (the corner group is complete). Continue round the

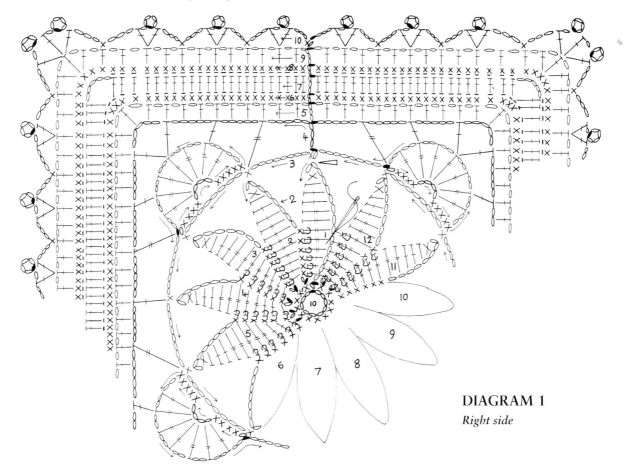

DIAGRAM 1
Right side

remaining sides, working 1ch sps and corner groups as before. Mark the centre tr of the corner groups for future reference. End with 1ch, miss 1ch, sl st to the 3rd of 4ch at the beginning of the round (22 x 1ch sps between the marked corners).

Note: Work all sts on rounds 6, 7 and 8 extra firmly.

Round 6   2ch, *1dc in sp, 1dc in tr, repeat from* till you reach the marked corner st, remove the marker, work 3dc in that st, replace the marker in the centre dc (under 2 threads). Continue to work from first* along the remaining sides. End with a sl st to 2ch at the beginning of the round.

Round 7   3ch (to count as 1tr), 1tr in each st, working into the **back single thread only**, till you reach the marked st, remove the marker,

work (1tr, 5ch, 1tr) in that corner st. Continue round the remaining sides, working 1tr in each st and (1tr, 5ch, 1tr) in the marked corner sts. End with a sl st to the 3rd of 3ch. There should be 47trs between the corner sps on each side. Adjust the number of sts, if and when necessary, it is important to have the correct stitch count on each side.

Round 8   2ch, *1dc in each st, work into the **back single thread only**, till you reach the corner 5ch sp, 5dc in corner sp, **mark** the centre dc of 5dc, repeat from*, till the remaining sides are complete.

Note: take care **not** to miss the first tr after 5dc in the corner. End with a sl st to 2ch.

Round 9   4ch, miss st at the base of 4ch and next st, 1tr in the next st (under **two** threads), *1ch, miss a st, 1tr in the next st, repeat from*

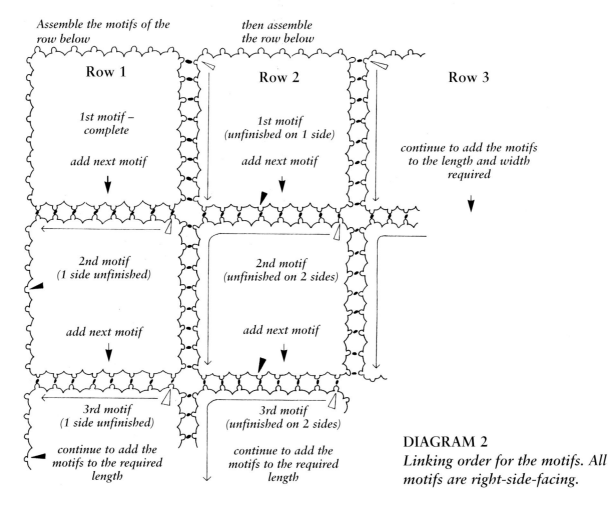

Assemble the motifs of the row below

then assemble the row below

Row 1

Row 2

Row 3

1st motif – complete

add next motif

1st motif (unfinished on 1 side)

add next motif

continue to add the motifs to the length and width required

2nd motif (1 side unfinished)

add next motif

2nd motif (unfinished on 2 sides)

add next motif

3rd motif (1 side unfinished)

continue to add the motifs to the required length

3rd motif (unfinished on 2 sides)

continue to add the motifs to the required length

DIAGRAM 2
Linking order for the motifs. All motifs are right-side-facing.

till 12sps made, remove marker, work 1ch, miss a st, (1tr, 1ch, 1tr, 1ch, 1tr) in corner st, replace marker in the centre tr of the corner group just made. Continue to work 1ch sps on the remaining sides, working the corner groups in the marked sts and placing the marker in the centre tr. End with a sl st to the 3rd of 4ch.

Note: There are 28 x 1ch sps between the marked corner trs.

Round 10   1ch, 1dc beside 1ch, *3ch, miss (1ch, 1tr, 1ch), work (1tr, 1 x 4ch picot, 1ch, 1tr) in next tr, 3ch, miss (1ch, 1tr, 1ch), 1dc (tight) in next tr, repeat from* 2 more times, 3ch, miss (1ch, 1tr, 1ch). Remove the marker, work a double picot group in the corner tr as follows: (1tr, 1 x 4ch picot, 1ch, 1tr, 1 x 4ch picot, 1ch, 1tr). **3ch, miss (1ch, 1tr, 1ch), 1dc in next tr, 3ch, miss (1ch, 1tr, 1ch), work (1tr, 1 x 4ch picot, 1ch, 1tr) in next tr, repeat from** along the remaining sides, working a double picot group in the corners as before. End with a

sl st to dc at the beginning of the round. Fasten off, sew in tail ends.

TO COMPLETE. Press lightly on the wrong side, using a steam iron and a damp cloth. Ease into shape. If necessary, pin out while still damp. Allow to dry. The first motif is now finished. Read the next paragraph carefully before completing the second motif.

LINKING THE MOTIFS
Refer to diagram 2, on page 92, for the linking order. With right side facing, start on the second motif. After completing round 9, proceed with round 10, but leave 1 complete side and the final half row unfinished, ending with the centre corner tr of the double picot group. Hold the loop with a safety pin and press the unfinished motif lightly on the wrong side before linking it. *Work 2ch of the next 4ch picot, insert the hook in the picot on the opposite motif (inserting the hook in the wrong side/back of the picot), sl st to link. Work the remaining 2ch

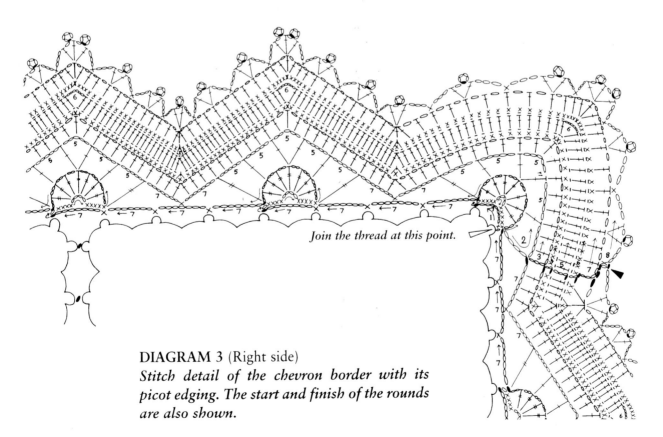

Join the thread at this point.

DIAGRAM 3 (Right side)
Stitch detail of the chevron border with its picot edging. The start and finish of the rounds are also shown.

of the picot and a sl st to the first of 4ch, 1ch, 1tr in same st as last tr, 3ch, miss (1ch, 1tr, 1ch), 1dc in next tr, 3ch, miss (1ch, 1tr, 1ch), 1tr in next tr, repeat from*, linking the motifs together till 8 picots have been crocheted together. Continue to complete the corner group and the last half row. End with a sl st to the dc at the beginning of the round. Fasten off.

Continue adding motifs in this way until you have obtained the required length, then begin to add the second row of motifs. When a motif is to be linked along **2** of its sides to another, remember to leave **2** sides, and the last half row of the third, unworked. The chevron border will fit any size or shape, square or oblong.

CHEVRON BORDER WITH A PICOT EDGE

Note: Marking the stitches at this stage is even more important as it will ensure a perfect finish.

Round 1   Right side facing. Join the thread by tying it to the right hand picot of the double picot group, as shown on diagram 3, page 93. Draw a working loop through as before, 1ch, 1dc beside 1ch. Work an open dtr 'shell' as follows: 7ch, sl st to the next picot, 1ch, **turn**, (4dc, 4ch, 4dc) in 7ch loop, 1dc in next dc, **turn**, 2ch, *1dtr in 4ch loop, 2ch, repeat from* 6 more times, miss 4dc, sl st in the next st (8 x 2ch sps made – or 1 open dtr 'shell'). **7ch, 1dc in the next picot, repeat from** till 3 x 7ch loops made. Work 1 open dtr 'shell' as before, repeat from** along the first full side, ending with 3 x 7ch loops before the next corner. Work 1 open dtr 'shell' over the next 2 corner picots. Now repeat the pattern sequence on the remaining 3 sides. End with a sl st to the dc at the beginning of the round. Do not turn.

Round 2   9ch (to count as 1dtr and 5ch), *miss (2ch, 1dtr, 2ch), 1tr in next dtr, 5ch, miss (2ch, 1dtr, 2ch), work (1tr, 5ch, 1tr) in next dtr, 5ch, miss (2ch, 1dtr, 2ch), 1tr in next dtr, 5ch, miss (2ch, 1dtr, 2ch), 1dtr in next st, **7ch**, miss (7ch, 1dc, 3ch), 1dc (tight) in next ch st, **7ch**, miss (3ch, 1dc, 7ch), 1dtr in dc at the beginning of the 'shell', 5ch, repeat from* along the first full side, work around corner and continue to repeat the pattern sequence on the remaining 3 sides. End the round by omitting the last dtr and working a sl st to the 4th of 9ch at the beginning of the round. Do not turn.

Note: Take extra care with this next round: mark each centre tr at all points for future reference.

Round 3   4ch (to count as 1tr and 1ch), miss st at base of 4ch, *1tr in next ch, 1ch, miss 1ch, 1tr in next ch, 1ch, miss 1ch, 1tr in next tr, 1ch, miss 1ch, repeat from* once more. Continue round the point as follows: 1tr in next ch, 1ch, 1tr in **next** ch, **mark** the tr just made. 1ch, 1tr in **next** ch, 1ch, miss 1ch, 1tr in next tr. Continue to work 1ch sps, missing 1ch between sts till 10 x 1ch sps are made from the marked tr, 1ch, miss 1ch, decrease next 2trs as follows: in next ch, work 1tr to the last stage but one (2 loops left on the hook), miss (1ch, 1dc, 1ch). In the next ch, work 1tr to the last stage but one (3 loops left on hook), yoh and draw through all 3 loops (decrease complete). Continue to repeat the pattern sequence, increasing and decreasing as required on the remaining 3 sides. End with a sl st to the 3rd of 4ch at the beginning of the round (23sps between marked trs). Do not turn.

Note: Work all sts on rounds 4, 5, 6 extra firmly.

Round 4   2ch, *1dc in sp, 1dc in tr, repeat from* till you reach the marked st, remove the marker, work 3dc in the next st, **mark** the centre dc, *1dc in sp, 1dc in tr, repeat from* till 21dc are made, from the marked dc (10sps from corner point). Decrease dc over the next 3sts as follows: insert the hook in the next sp, draw the thread through, hook in the next st, draw the thread through, hook in the next sp, draw the thread through (4 loops now on hook), yoh and draw through all 4 loops on the hook (3dc decrease complete).

Note: You may find it useful to mark under the top 2 threads of decrease for future reference. Continue st sequence, 1dc in tr, 1dc in sp, increasing and decreasing, replacing the markers as required. Refer to diagram 3. End with a sl st to 2ch. Do not turn.

Round 5 3ch, 1tr in each st, working into the **back single thread only**, till you reach the marked st at the point (see diagram), * remove the marker, work (1tr, 6ch, 1tr) in that st, work 1tr in each st till 21sts are made, from 6ch sp. Decrease the next 2trs as follows: work 1tr in next st to the last stage but one (2 loops on hook), **miss** the marked st (decrease on the row before), work 1tr in the next st to the last stage but one (3 loops on hook), yoh and draw through all 3 loops on the hook (2tr decrease is complete). Work 1tr in each next 20 sts. Continue to repeat the pattern sequence from* on the remaining sides. End with 1tr in each of the remaining 3sts after the **last** 2tr decrease, sl st to 3rd of 3ch. Do not turn, (22trs between decrease and increase markers). Check your work frequently to keep the stitch count accurate and adjust if necessary.

Round 6 2ch, 1dc in each st, working into the **back single thread only**, till you reach the corner sp (17dc), *7dc in 6ch loop, **mark** the centre dc of 7dc, 1dc in each st till 23 dc from the marked corner dc, decrease the next 3dc, 1dc in each next 20sts till you reach the corner sp. Continue to repeat the pattern sequence from* on the remaining sides. End with 1dc in each remaining 2sts after **last** 3dc decrease, sl st to the second of 2ch, **sl st again** in next dc. Do not turn.

Round 7... 4ch, miss st at the base of 4ch and next st, 1tr in next st, (under **2** threads), *1ch,

miss a st, 1tr in next st, repeat from* till 9sps made, 1ch, miss a st, remove marker, work (1tr, 1ch, 1tr, 1ch, 1tr) in stitch at point, replace the marker in the centre tr of the corner group. **1ch, miss a st, 1tr in next st, repeat from** till 11 sps from marked st are made, 1ch, miss a st, decrease next 3trs as follows: work 1tr in next st to the last stage but one, **miss 1dc**, 1tr in next st to the last stage but one, **miss 1dc**, 1tr in the next st to the last stage but one, yoh and draw through all 4 loops on hook, **mark** this decrease for future reference. Continue to repeat the pattern sequence, checking the diagram to ensure the correct placing of the increases / decreases and of the space count between the marked sts. The space count from here will be 12 x 1ch sps between increase and decrease markers. Complete all sides, including the last 3tr decrease on the last side. End with 1ch, a sl st to the 3rd of 3ch, a sl st **again** in the next ch and the next tr. 1ch. Do not turn.

Round 8 1dc beside 1ch, *3ch, miss (1ch, 1tr, 1ch), work (1tr, 1 x 4ch picot, 1ch, 1tr) in the next tr, 3ch, miss (1ch, 1tr, 1ch), 1dc (tightly) in the next tr, repeat from* once more. 3ch, miss (1ch, 1tr 1ch), remove the marker, work a double picot group in the corner tr as follows: (1tr, 1 x 4ch picot, 1ch, 1tr, 1 x 4ch picot, 1ch, 1tr). Continue to repeat the pattern sequence on the remaining sides till the last single picot group is complete. End with 3ch, miss 1ch, sl st to dc at the beginning of the round. Fasten off, sew in tail ends.

TO COMPLETE
Press lightly on the wrong side, using a damp cloth. Ease gently into shape on a flat surface, covered in cling film. Allow to dry.

SCOTTISH THISTLE DOILY

Approximate size: 16 in / 41 cm square

MATERIALS. 90 g DMC Cébélia crochet cotton No 10 – white 5200, a 1.50 mm crochet hook

STITCHES, ABBREVIATIONS & SYMBOLS

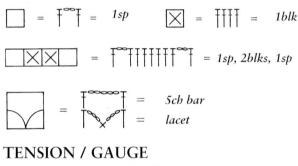

TENSION / GAUGE

WORKING NOTES

- 2ch between trs on open mesh
- Work in same direction on each round, following the stitch diagrams as you work.
- Keep the tension firm and even throughout.
- 3ch at the start of a round count as 1tr.
- 5ch at the start of a round count as 1tr and 2ch.

BEGIN. (See diagram 1 on page 98), 9ch, sl st to form a ring.

Round 1 5ch, 1tr in ring, *5ch, 1tr in ring, 2ch, 1tr in ring, repeat from* 2 more times, 5ch, sl st to the 3rd of 5ch. Do not turn.

Round 2 3ch, 2tr in 2ch sp, 1tr in tr, 2ch, *(1tr, 5ch, 1tr) in the centre ch of 5ch, 2ch, miss 2ch, 1tr in tr, 2tr in 2ch sp, 1tr in tr, 2ch, miss 2ch, repeat from* 2 more times. End with (1tr, 5ch, 1tr) in the centre ch of 5ch, 2ch, miss 2ch, sl st to the 3rd of 3ch.

Round 3 3ch, 1tr in each next 3tr, *3ch, miss 2ch, 1dc (tightly) in next tr, 3ch, miss 2ch, (1tr, 5ch, 1tr) in the centre ch of 5ch, 3ch, miss 2ch, 1dc in next tr, 3ch, miss 2ch, 1tr in each next 4tr, repeat from* 2 more times. End with 3ch, miss 2ch, 1dc in next tr, 3ch, miss 2ch, (1tr, 5ch, 1tr) in the centre ch of 5ch, 3ch, miss 2ch, 1dc (tightly) in next tr, 3ch, sl st to the 3rd of 3ch.

Round 4 to round 33 Follow diagram 2 on page 98, working blocks and spaces. **Remember the rule:** if there is a **block** at the beginning of the round, work 3ch, 2tr in sp or in **trs**, 1tr in next tr. If there is a **space** at the beginning of the round, work 5ch, miss **2ch** or **2trs**, 1tr in next tr. End round 33 with a sl st to the 3rd of 5ch.

Note: Every few rounds, check to make sure that the work lies reasonably flat. If **not**, re-work from where the 'waving' begins, and keep the tension consiste\nt throughout.

FINAL EDGE. Follow diagram 3 on page 99 for stitch detail.

Round 34 3ch, 2tr in sp, 1tr in next tr, *3ch, miss 2ch, 1dc in next tr, 3ch, miss 2ch, 1tr in tr,

DIAGRAM 1
(Right side)

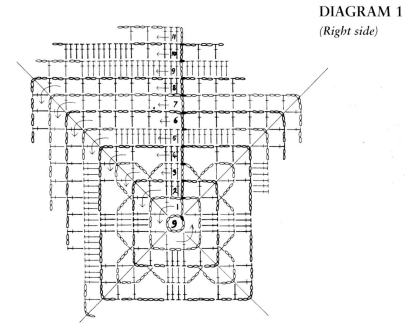

DIAGRAM 2
(Right side)

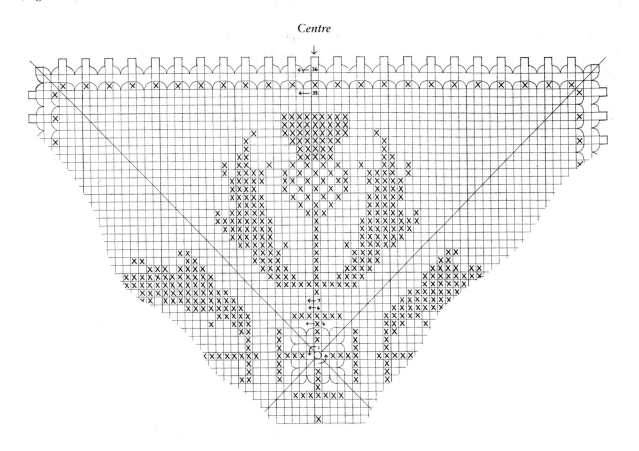

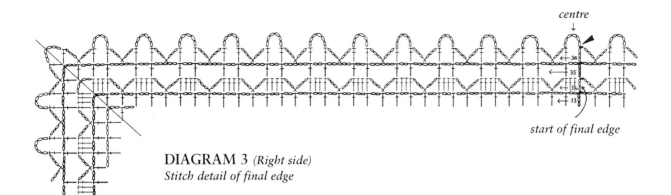

centre

start of final edge

DIAGRAM 3 *(Right side)*
Stitch detail of final edge

2tr in sp, 1tr in next tr, repeat from* till 11 x 4tr blks are complete, 3ch, miss 2ch, 1dc in next tr, 3ch, miss 2ch, 1tr in next tr, (3tr, 5ch, 3tr) in 5ch corner loop, 1tr in next tr. Continue to work the remaining sides and the corners as before, following the diagram. End with a sl st to the 3rd of 3ch at the beginning of the round.

Round 35   5ch, miss 2tr, 1tr in next tr, *5ch, miss (3ch, 1dc, 3ch), 1tr in tr, 2ch, miss 2tr, 1tr in tr, repeat from* till you reach the corner sp. Work 2ch, (1tr, 5ch, 1tr) in the centre ch of 5ch, 2ch, 1tr in tr, 2ch, miss 2tr, 1tr in tr. Continue to work the remaining sides and corners as before. End with 5ch, sl st to the 3rd of 5ch at the beginning of the round.

Round 36   9ch, to count as 1tr and 6ch, miss 2ch, 1tr in next tr*, 3ch, miss 2ch, 1dc (tightly) in next ch, 3ch, miss 2ch, 1tr in next tr, 6ch, miss 2ch, 1tr in next tr, repeat from* till 12 x 6ch loops have been made, 3ch, miss 2ch, 1dc in next tr, 3ch, (1tr, 6ch, 1tr) in the centre ch of 5ch, 3ch, miss 2ch, 1tr in next tr. Continue to work the remaining sides and corners as before, till you have worked the last 6ch loop and 1tr in tr. End with 3ch, miss 2ch, 1dc in next ch, 3ch, miss 2ch, sl st to the 3rd of 9ch at the beginning of the round. Fasten off, sew in tail ends.

TO COMPLETE. Press lightly on the wrong side, using a damp cloth. To make sure that the doily is absolutely square, draw a square on a piece of paper. Place it on a board and cover it with cling film. Finally, pin the doily on to the board, using the drawn shape to guide you. Allow to dry fully.

Overleaf. The Scottish thistle doily

FILIGREE LACE DOILY

Approximate size: 11 in x 9 in / 28 x 23 cm

MATERIALS. 20 g DMC Cébélia crochet cotton No 10 – pale yellow 745 or white 5200, a 1.50 mm crochet hook

SPECIAL STITCHES

5ch bar
lacet

WORKING NOTES

◆ Written instructions are given for the first few rounds to familiarise you with the 'bar and lacet' technique. The complete pattern is shown in the diagram on page 102.

◆ Photocopy this diagram, colouring in each round lightly as you work.

◆ The increases appear in bold (darker lines) on the diagram.

◆ Work in the same direction throughout (right side facing). All chs and sts must be firm and even.

◆ Mark the 3rd ch of the starting chain as you begin each round as a guide to the correct placing of the sl st at the **end** of each round. Remove and replace the markers as required.

BEGIN. 29ch.

Round 1   1tr in 8th ch from hook, *2ch, miss 2ch, 1tr in next ch, repeat from* till 7 x 2ch spaces made, 2ch, miss 2ch, (1tr, 2ch) 5 times in the last ch. This will have turned your work (still with right side facing) ready to work along the underside of the foundation chain. Continue: miss 2ch, *1tr in next ch, 2ch, miss 2ch, repeat from* 6 more times, (1tr, 2ch) 4 times in next ch. End by missing 1ch, sl st to next ch at the beginning of the round (see diagram).

Round 2   6ch (to count as 1tr and 3ch), miss 2ch, 1dc in next tr, 3ch, miss 2ch, 1tr in next tr (the first lacet is made), work the next lacet as follows: *(3ch, miss 2ch, 1dc in next tr, 3ch, miss 2ch, 1tr in next tr), repeat from* till 5 lacets are made, work 3ch, 1tr in the same tr as last tr, repeat from* again, along other side till another 6 lacets are made, 3ch, 1tr in the same tr as the last tr, 3ch, miss 2ch, 1dc in next tr, 3ch, miss 2ch. End with a sl st into 3rd of 6ch at the beginning of the round.

Round 3   8ch (to count as 1tr and 1 x 5ch bar), miss (3ch, 1dc, 3ch), 1tr in next tr, *5ch, miss (3ch, 1dc, 3ch), 1tr in next tr (2nd 5ch bar is made), repeat from* till 4 bars are made, 3ch, 1tr in same tr as last tr, 5ch, miss (3ch, 1dc, 3ch), work (1tr, 3ch, 1tr) in next tr, 3ch, miss 3ch, (1tr, 3ch, 1tr) in next tr, 5ch, miss (3ch, 1dc, 3ch), work (1tr, 3ch, 1tr) in next tr, **5ch, miss (3ch, 1dc, 3ch), 1tr in next tr, repeat from** 3 more times, 3ch, 1tr in same tr as last tr, 5ch, miss (3ch, 1dc, 3ch), work (1tr, 3ch, 1tr) in next tr, 3ch, miss 3ch, (1tr, 3ch, 1tr) in next tr, 5ch, miss (3ch, 1dc, 3ch), 1tr at the base of 8ch, end with 3ch, sl st to the 3rd of 8ch.

NOTE: (1tr, 3ch, 1tr) worked in the same stitch is an increase (8 increases on round 3).

Round 4 6ch (to count as 1tr and 3ch), miss 2ch, 1dc in next ch, 3ch, miss 2ch, 1tr in next tr (lacet made), *3ch, miss 2ch, 1dc in next ch, 3ch, miss 2ch, 1tr in next tr, repeat from* 2 more times, 5ch, miss 3ch, 1tr in next tr, 3ch, miss 2ch, 1dc in next ch, 3ch, miss 2ch, 1tr in next tr, 5ch, miss 3ch, 1tr in next tr, 3ch, miss 3ch, 1tr in next tr, 5ch, miss 3ch, 1tr in next tr, 3ch, miss 2ch, 1dc in next ch, 3ch, miss 2ch, 1tr in next tr, 5ch, miss 3ch, 1tr in next tr, *3ch, miss 2ch, 1dc in next ch, 3ch, miss 2ch, 1tr in next tr, repeat from* 3 more times, 5ch, miss 3ch, 1tr in next tr, 3ch, miss 2ch, 1dc in next ch, 3ch, miss 2ch, 1tr in next tr, 5ch, miss 3ch, 1tr in next tr, 3ch, miss 3ch, 1tr in next tr, 5ch, miss 3ch, 1tr in next tr, 3ch, miss 2ch, 1dc in next ch, 3ch, miss 2ch, 1tr in next tr. End with 5ch, miss 3ch, sl st to 3rd of 6ch. You may find it useful to tie a contrasting thread around the 3ch at each end of the oval on round 4 (see diagram). These markers can be left in till the doily is complete

Filigree doily (right side)

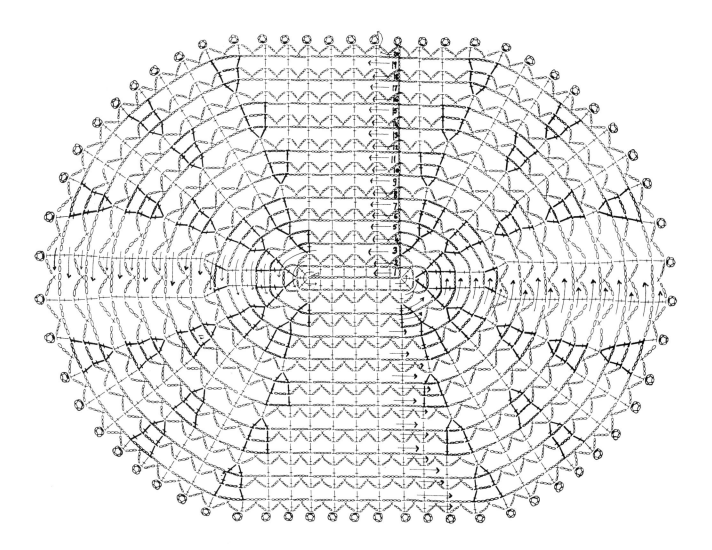

102

Round 5 to round 20 Continue, following the stitch diagram. Take extra care at all stages: the correct placing of the increases, marked in bold on the diagram, is vital. As each round becomes bigger, the stitch arrangement around each end of the oval shape changes slightly.

Detail for round 20: 8ch, sl st to 5th ch from hook (making 1 x 5ch picot), 3ch, miss 2ch, 1dc in next ch, 3ch, miss 2ch, *(1tr, 1 x 5ch picot) in next tr, 3ch, miss 2ch, 1dc in next ch, 3ch, miss 2ch, repeat from* till round. End with a sl st to the 3rd of 8ch at the beginning of the round. Fasten off, sew in tail ends.

TO COMPLETE
Press lightly on the wrong side, using a damp cloth. Ease gently into shape, over a board covered in cling film, pinning out the picots evenly all round.

Below. The filigree doily worked in white. Overleaf. The yellow version of the filigree doily.

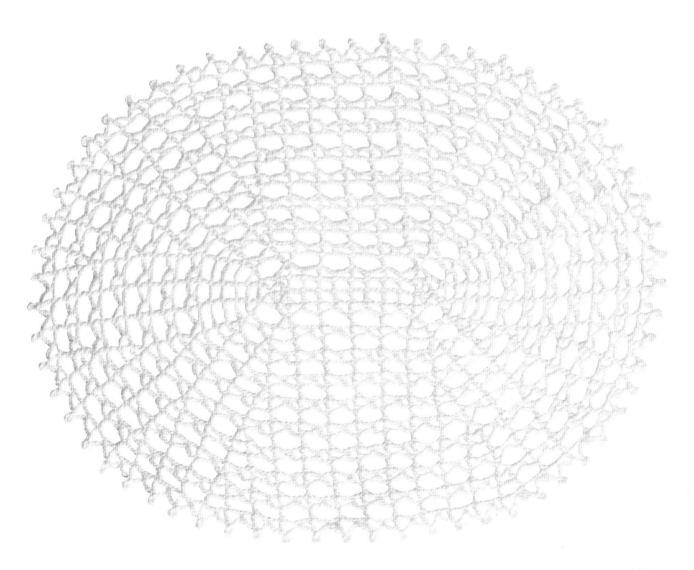

AUTUMN LEAVES DOILY

Approximate size: 8½ in / 22 cm in diameter

MATERIALS. 20 g DMC Cébélia crochet cotton No 10 – écru 712 or white 5200, a 1.50 mm crochet hook

WORKING NOTES
◆ 3ch at the beginning of the round count as 1tr.
◆ Make a photocopy of the diagram on page 106 and colour each round as you work.
◆ Work in the same direction on each round and tighten all chs, dcs and trs as you finish each st.

BEGIN. 10ch, sl st to form a ring.

Round 1 3ch (to count as 1tr), 23tr, in the ring (24tr including 3ch), sl st to the 3rd of 3ch, do not turn.

Round 2 1ch, 1dc beside 1ch, 5ch, *miss 2tr, 1dc in next tr, 5ch, repeat from* till round. End with a sl st in the first dc at the beginning of the round (8 x 5ch loops made). Sl st in each next 3ch of the first 5ch loop.

Round 3 8ch, *1dc in the next 5ch loop, 8ch, repeat from* till round. End with a sl st to the first ch of 8ch, sl st **again** in next ch.

Round 4 3ch, 10trs in first loop, 11tr in each next 7 loops. End with a sl st to the 3rd of 3ch at the beginning of the round (8 x 11tr groups made). From now on, mark the start of each round.

Round 5 6ch (to count as 1tr and 3ch), 1tr in the space directly below 6ch, 5ch, 1dc (tightly) in the centre tr of the 11tr group, 5ch, miss 5tr *(1tr, 3ch, 1tr) in the space between the next two 11tr groups, 5ch, miss 5tr, 1dc (tightly) in next tr, 5ch, miss 5tr, repeat from* till round. End with a sl st to the 3rd of 6ch.

Round 6 3ch, 4tr in 3ch space, 3ch, 1dc in 5ch loop, 3ch, 1dc in next 5ch loop, 3ch, *5tr in 3ch space, 3ch, 1dc in 5ch loop, 3ch, 1dc in next 5ch loop, 3ch, repeat from* till round. End with a sl st to the 3rd of 3ch.

Round 7 3ch, 1tr in the st at the base of 3ch, 1tr in each next 3tr, 2tr in next tr, 5ch, miss 3ch, 1dc in next 3ch loop, 5ch, miss next 3ch, *2tr in next tr, 1tr in each next 3tr, 2tr in next tr, 5ch, miss 3ch, 1dc in next 3ch loop, 5ch, miss 3ch, repeat from* till round. End with a sl st to the 3rd of 3ch.

Round 8 3ch, 1tr in st at the base of 3ch, 1tr in each next 5tr, 2tr in next tr, 3ch, 1dc in 5ch loop, 3ch, 1dc in next 5ch loop, 3ch, *2tr in next tr, 1tr in each next 5tr, 2tr in next tr, 3ch, 1dc in the 5ch loop, 3ch, 1dc in the next 5ch loop, 3ch, repeat from* till round. End with a sl st to the 3rd of 3ch.

Round 9 3ch, 1tr in each next 6tr, decrease last 2tr, 7ch, miss 3ch, 1dc in next 3ch loop, 7ch, miss 3ch, *decrease next 2tr, 1tr in each next **5tr**, decrease next 2tr, 7ch, miss 3ch, 1dc in next 3ch loop, 7ch, miss 3ch, repeat from* till round.

End with a sl st in the first tr at the beginning of the round, **not** the 3ch.

Round 10 3ch, 1tr in each next 4tr, decrease next 2tr, 5ch, 1dc in 7ch loop, 5ch, 1dc in next 7ch loop, 5ch, *decrease next 2tr, 1tr in each next **3tr,** decrease next 2tr, 5ch, 1dc in 7ch loop, 5ch, 1dc in next 7ch loop, 5ch, repeat from* till round. End with a sl st in the first tr, **not** the 3ch.

Round 11 3ch, 1tr in each next 2tr, decrease next 2tr, 5ch, 1dc in 5ch loop, 5ch, 5tr in next 5ch loop, 5ch, 1dc in next 5ch loop, 5ch, decrease next 2tr, **1tr** in next tr, decrease next 2tr, 5ch, 1dc in 5ch loop, 5ch, continue with the stitch sequence as shown on diagram till round.

End with a sl st to the first tr, **not** the 3ch.

Round 12 3ch, decrease next 2tr, 3ch, 1dc in 5ch loop, 3ch, 1dc in the next 5ch loop, 3ch, 2tr in first tr, 1tr in each next 3tr, 2tr in next tr, 3ch, 1dc in 5ch loop, 3ch, 1dc in next 5ch loop, 3ch, decrease next 3tr, 3ch, 1dc in 5ch loop, 3ch, 1dc in next 5ch loop, 3ch, continue the stitch sequence as shown on the diagram till round. End with a sl st to the first tr, **not** the 3ch.

Round 13 8ch (to count as 1tr and 5ch), miss 3ch, 1dc in next loop, 5ch, miss 3ch, 2tr in first tr, 1tr in each next 5tr, 2tr in next tr, 5ch, miss 3ch, 1dc in next 3ch loop, 5ch, miss 3ch, 1tr in st on top of 3tr decrease, 5ch, miss 3ch, 1dc in

Doily (right side)

next 3ch loop, 5ch continue the stitch sequence as shown on the diagram till the end of the round. End with a sl st to the 3rd of 8ch.

Round 14 6ch (to count as 1tr and 3ch), 1tr in st at base of 6ch, 5ch, miss 5ch, 1dc in next 5ch loop, 5ch, decrease next 2tr, 1tr in each next 5tr, decrease next 2tr, 5ch, 1dc in 5ch loop, 5ch, miss 5ch, (1tr, 3ch, 1tr) in tr, 5ch, miss 5ch, 1dc in next 5ch loop, 5ch, continue the stitch sequence as shown on diagram till the end of the round. End with a sl st to the 3rd of 6ch.

Round 15 3ch, 1tr in st at base of 3ch, 5ch, miss 3ch, 2tr in next tr, 5ch, miss 5ch, 1dc in next 5ch loop, 5ch, decrease next 2tr, 1tr in each next 3tr, decrease next 2tr, 5ch, 1dc in 5ch loop, 5ch, miss 5ch, 2tr in next tr, 5ch, miss 3ch, 2tr in next tr, 5ch, miss 5ch, 1dc in next 5ch loop, 5ch, continue the stitch sequence as shown on diagram till the end of the round. End with a sl st to the 3rd of 3ch.

Round 16 3ch, 1tr in next tr, 3ch, miss 2ch, 2tr in next **ch st**, 3ch, miss 2ch, 1tr in each next 2tr, 5ch, miss 5ch, 1dc in next 5ch loop, 5ch, decrease next 2tr, 1tr in next tr, decrease next 2tr, 5ch, 1dc in next 5ch loop, 5ch, miss 5ch, 1tr in each next 2tr, continue the stitch sequence as shown on diagram till the end of the round. End with a sl st to the 3rd of 3ch.

Round 17 3ch, 1tr in next tr, 5ch, miss 3ch, 1tr in each next 2tr, 5ch, miss 3ch, 1tr in each next

2tr, 5ch, miss 5ch, 1dc in next 5ch loop, 5ch, decrease next 3tr, 5ch, 1dc in next 5ch loop, 5ch, miss 5ch, 1tr in each next 2tr, continue the stitch sequence as shown on diagram till the end of the round. End with a sl st to the 3rd of 3ch.

Round 18 3ch, 1tr in next tr, **6ch**, miss 5ch, 1tr in each 2tr, **6ch**, miss 5ch, 1tr in each next 2tr, **5ch**, miss 5ch, 1dc in next 5ch loop, **3ch**, 1tr in st on top of 3tr decrease, **3ch**, 1dc in next 5ch loop, **5ch**, miss 5ch, 1tr in each next 2tr, **6ch**, miss 5ch, continue the stitch sequence as shown on diagram till the end of the round. End with a sl st to the 3rd of 3ch.

Round 19 7ch, sl st in 4th ch from hook (this counts as 1tr and 1 x 4ch picot), 1ch, 1tr in next tr, 3ch, 1dc in 6ch loop, 3ch, 1tr in next tr, 1 x 4ch picot, 1ch, 1tr in next tr, 3ch, 1dc in 6ch loop, 3ch, 1tr in next tr, 1 x 4ch picot, 1ch, 1tr in next tr, 3ch, 1dc in 5ch loop, 3ch, miss 3ch, (1tr, 1 x 4ch picot, 1ch, 1tr, 1 x 4ch picot, 1ch, 1tr, 1 x 4ch picot, 1ch, 1tr) in next tr, 3ch, miss 3ch, 1dc in next 5ch loop, 3ch, continue the stitch sequence as shown on diagram till the end of the round. End with a sl st to the 3rd of 7ch at the beginning of the round. Fasten off, sew in tail ends.

TO COMPLETE. Press lightly on the wrong side, using a damp cloth. Ease gently into shape over a board covered in cling film, pinning out the picots evenly all round.

EQUIVALENT ENGLISH AND AMERICAN TERMS

English
Double crochet (dc)
Half treble (htr)
Treble (tr)
Double treble (dtr)
Triple treble (ttr)
Yarn over hook (yoh)

Cast off
Miss
Tension
Work straight

American
Single crochet (sc)
Half double crochet (hdc)
Double crochet (dc)
Triple crochet (trc)
Double treble (dtr)
Yarn over hook (yo)

Fasten off
Skip
Gauge
Work even

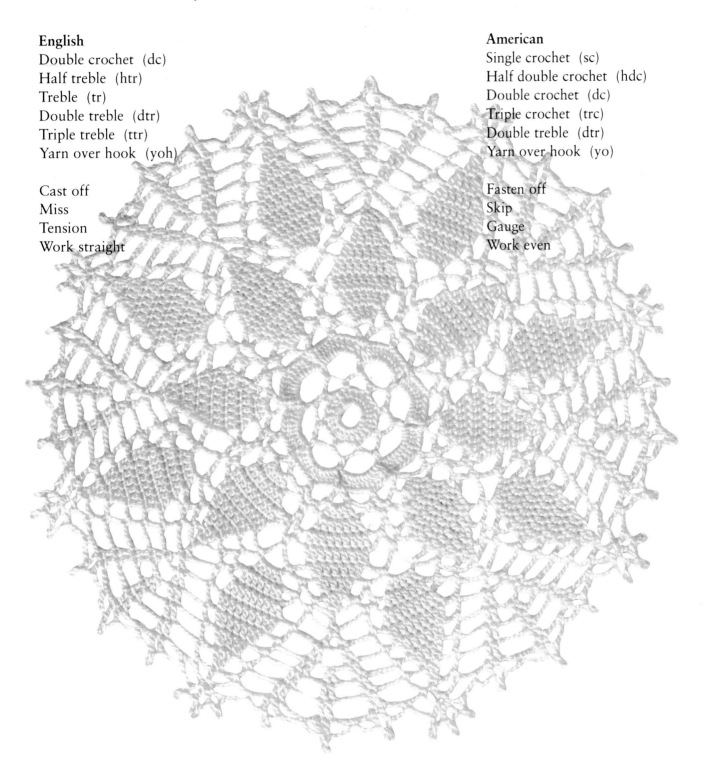